The *Life* Of The Party

The *Life* Of The Party

A True Story Of Teenage Alcoholism

Becky Tirabassi with Gregg Lewis

A DIVISION OF CTi
CampusLife BOOKS / Zondervan Publishing House
Grand Rapids, Michigan

The Life of the Party
Copyright © 1987, 1990 by Campus Life Books,
a division of CTi
All rights reserved.

Previously published as **Just One Victory** by Tyndale House Publishers Inc., Wheaton, Illinois.

Published by Zondervan
Publishing House
1415 Lake Drive, S.E.,
Grand Rapids, Michigan 49506

This story is based on true life. The names of people and places have been changed to protect all those mentioned.

"Just One Victory" by Todd Rundgren. From the LP "A Wizard, A True Star." Released by Bearsville Records, Inc., 1973. Copyright/publishing: Fiction music, Inc.—25%; Todd Rundgren—25%; Screen Gems Music—50%.

Library of Congress Cataloging-in-Publication Data

Tirabassi, Becky, 1954–
    (Just one victory)
    The life of the party / Becky Tirabassi with Gregg Lewis.
      p. cm.
    Reprint. Originally published: Just one victory. 1987.
    ISBN 0-310-71081-2
    1. Tirabassi, Becky, 1954–. 2. Christian biography—United States. 3. Alcoholics—United States—Biography. 4. Teenage girls—United States—Alcohol use. I. Lewis, Gregg A. II. Title.
    BR1725.T57A3   1990
    248.8'6'092—dc20   90–41282
    (B)   CIP

All rights reserved. No part of this publication may be reproduced, stored in a retrieval system, or transmitted in any form or by any means—electronic, mechanical, photocopy, recording, or any other—except for brief quotations in printed reviews, without the prior permission of the publisher.

Printed in the United States of America

90 91 92 93 94 / CH / 5 4 3 2 1

To Roger, Jake, Mom, Dad, Rick, Wendy, and Kinney—whose love, support, and encouragement have made this book possible.

Campus Life Books

Against All Odds
Alive
Alive II
The Campus Life Guide to Dating
The Campus Life Guide to Making
  and Keeping Friends
The Campus Life Guide to
  Surviving High School
The Life of the Party
The Lighter Side of Campus Life
A Love Story
Peer Pressure: Making It Work for
  You
What Teenagers Are Saying About
  Drugs and Alcohol
Worth the Wait
You Call This a Family?

CONTENTS

Chapter 1.	"I Won't Be a Nobody!"	9
Chapter 2.	My Secret Weapon	21
Chapter 3.	Life of the Party	29
Chapter 4.	Trouble Hits	39
Chapter 5.	Fighting for Control	51
Chapter 6.	A New Start	61
Chapter 7.	Losing Ground	71
Chapter 8.	California Crossroads	81
Chapter 9.	Pursuing the Victory	91
Chapter 10.	Searching for Love	101
Chapter 11.	"I Think I'm an Alcoholic!"	113
Chapter 12.	One Real Victory	125
Chapter 13.	In Different Worlds	133
Chapter 14.	Going Home	143
	Epilogue	151
	A Final Word from Becky	157
	If You Prayed That Prayer . . .	160

CHAPTER 1

"I WON'T BE A NOBODY!"

*P*eople always act surprised when they hear all the things that have happened to me. Indeed, there were many times when I felt I was the only teenager in the world who felt the way I did, who went through what I did in high school and the four years that followed.

And yet, almost every time I'm asked to tell my experiences in front of a group, someone will come up afterward and say, "I know exactly what you went through," "That happened to my sister," or "When you were talking, I realized you could have been me."

So while I now realize my life may have taken some unusual twists and turns, I've come to understand that what happened to me and why it happened aren't unusual at all. However, it is my story. And it really began the first day I got off the bus in front of Grove Junior High School.

The two-story, limestone-brick building seemed to tower over me. Countless windows reflected the late summer sky and testified to the presence of more classrooms, more teachers, and more kids than I'd ever imagined in one school.

I walked hesitantly but excitedly up the semicircular driveway as bus after bus disgorged a stream of boisterous junior highers. Passing through those open front doors, I found myself being swept along in a surging river of humanity.

The first feeling that struck me was fear. A cold, gnawing sense in the pit of my stomach told me I didn't belong. While everyone else knew each other, I was alone. Although this was the first day of the school year, everyone else seemed to know the routine. Everyone else had a comfortable little niche, but I was a displaced stranger, hopelessly caught in the crowded hallway current and about to be sucked into a terrifying black hole of anonymity.

My second feeling was one of determination. I would do whatever it took to avoid anonymity and to rid myself of that terrible fear.

It didn't take long to learn the foolproof recipe for instant popularity in my new school. The trouble was that I didn't have enough of the right ingredients.

As in every school, the cutest kids were popular. They had distinctive looks, gorgeous hair, engaging smiles. I wore my straight, dull brown hair short, my ugly brown glasses shielded my eyes, and I couldn't smile without revealing my braces. So I knew I couldn't count on my looks for popularity.

I noticed right away that the popular kids tended to be sharp dressers—the ones with the sophisticated, fashionable clothes. I immediately determined to trade my elementary-school look for the trendier look of *Seventeen* magazine and more importantly, the ninth-grade in-group. By the end of the first week of school I'd begged and badgered my mother until she took me to the biggest department store in Chicago and bought me some new clothes. But all I got was a couple of new outfits because that's all my mom said she and Dad could afford right then—which leads me to another ingredient of popularity.

The popular kids seemed to be the kids with the most money, who lived in the ritziest subdivision and had gone to the nicest and newest elementary school. I lived in a modest house; we weren't poor, but we didn't have much excess money sitting around after the bills were paid each month. So I could never afford to take dance classes or join in the other little extracurricular activities the popular kids seemed to do.

Yet another popularity factor I had no control over was parents. The popular kids seemed to have great parents who were totally permissive, paying for big parties and generally encouraging their kids to get involved in the social scene. In short, other kids' parents seemed pretty with it, plus a lot of them seemed to know one another and to socialize frequently.

My mom and dad, on the other hand, thought I was too young to be wearing nylons, using makeup, or piercing my ears. Because they were ten to twelve years older than most of my classmates' parents, they socialized with a different, older crowd—people with grown children like my sister and brother, who were eleven and seven years older than I. As a result, my dad and mom seemed almost totally out of touch with my world. While they thought I was too young when I tried to look more adult, they thought I was too old when I just wanted to be a kid.

That's why we had the biggest fight of my life that Halloween. All my seventh-grade friends and all the kids I wanted to be friends with were planning to have a big party and go trick-or-treating. My mom told me I couldn't go.

"You're too old for trick-or-treating," she said.

"But everyone else is go—"

"You're not 'everyone.' And you're not going!" she said.

I didn't give up. I reasoned and argued. I cried. Finally I screamed and yelled with such ferocity that I was surprised almost as much as my parents. But they didn't budge. And I felt certain that the fun and opportunity I missed that night set my social life back so far that now I'd have to work even harder for popularity. Despite my parents and all the other factors I couldn't change, I saw some strategies I thought could improve my chances.

I did everything in my power to be where the popular kids were. For example, I turned down the opportunity to take honors courses because I didn't want to be seen as one of the books-and-brains set. The most popular kids were in the mainstream classes, so that's where I wanted to be. I spent hours writing notes in class, consulting with my friends about what we'd wear the next day. I spent more hours on the phone calling the right people; making plans for parties, sleepovers, and football games; gossiping about particular boys I liked in hopes that the word would spread.

While I never felt I achieved the popularity I longed for during seventh grade, I did see how I could attain it for the next year. I would become a cheerleader. The cheerleaders were undeniably the most popular girls in the school. When tryout time came in the spring, I'd be there. I'd win a spot on next year's cheerleading squad, and I'd be popular beyond my wildest dreams. From the time I set that goal early in the fall of my seventh-grade year, I lived for that day. I went to every ball game and studied the routines. I practiced at home in my room by the hour. When my chance came, I was going to be ready.

Almost ninety girls showed up for the junior high school tryouts that spring, all vying for eight spots on the next year's squad. And if those odds weren't bad enough, the coach told us only one or two seventh graders would be selected; the rest of the spots would go to eighth graders.

Even so, I felt I had a good chance. Waiting and watching there in the gym as other girls performed for the panel of teachers and coaches who would pick the squad, I knew I was ready. Of all the other seventh graders trying out, I felt certain my toughest competition would come from Kim Calkins. Not only was Kim pretty and athletic, she had the advantage of years of gymnastics and dance classes. *But, I told myself, I have the advantage of enthusiasm and determination.*

When my turn came, I gave it my all. In no time my tryout was over, the panel thanked me, and I went home, hoping against hope that my all had been enough.

I lay in bed that night, staring at the familiar shadows of my darkened room, unable to sleep. A slow-motion replay of my tryout ran over and over through my memory. I tried to analyze every move I had made. I tried to interpret every expression on the judges' faces. And I wondered if the next morning, my personal judgment day, would ever come.

I thought back to my elementary school years when I had

gone with my parents to every high school football game to watch my brother play. Fred had been the captain of the team, so, of course, he had dated the captain of the cheerleading squad. I'd stood on the sidelines screaming out the cheers along with the cheerleaders, dreaming of the day when I would be out there in front of the crowd, dating the quarterback, being liked by everyone. That's what I'd always wanted. Now more than ever.

Lying there in bed, I even bargained with God. "Lord," I prayed, "if you'll just let me make the cheerleading squad, I promise I'll cheerfully obey my parents. I'll pay closer attention in confirmation class. I'll pray more. I'll be a good girl. Please just let me make the squad."

Sleep finally came. And, of course, morning quickly followed. With it came homeroom period—the time for daily announcements. I sat at my desk, oblivious to everything around me. A dozen times I looked up from my mindless doodling to make sure the PA speaker still hung on the wall above the teacher's desk. Finally, the intercom crackled with static and the principal's voice boomed out: "We'd like to congratulate the following members of next year's Grove Junior High cheerleading squad." Then he started reading the names, beginning with the girls who would be ninth graders next year.

I waited for my name to be read at the very end. But as the tension mounted inside me, I lost count of the number of names already called until I heard the words I was listening for: "And the only eighth grader on next year's squad will be"—the pause seemed eternal—"Kim Calkins."

In that instant all my dreams for the coming year were crushed. I was sentenced to another twelve months as a mere spectator of school life. I'd have to be an eighth-grade nobody just like I'd been a seventh-grade nobody. And there was no one I could tell how much I hurt.

As things turned out, eighth grade wasn't a total loss. I got involved in sports, playing field hockey and girls' basketball. I even served on the student council and got elected as an officer of the Girls' Athletic Association (GAA). I made a lot of friends and had a blast in GAA. The cabinet would sometimes get together for overnights at our P.E. teacher's house, and it was there I remember my first serious discussions about the subject of sex. I was pretty naive: "My parents have had three kids. Does that mean," I asked, "they had sex three times?"

My P.E. teacher laughed so hard I thought she was going to fall out of her chair. So did all the other girls, most of whom were older ninth graders.

I'm not sure they realized my question was serious. I laughed along with them and pretended it wasn't. But it didn't really matter. I enjoyed being the life of the party and making everyone laugh, intentionally or accidentally. In fact, I was earning a reputation in school and out as something of a cutup. I'd often stand up in class and mimic a teacher whose back was turned. And when the class would erupt with laughter, I would drop into my seat and adopt the most innocent expression imaginable the split second before the teacher turned around.

But what I really lived for was another shot at real popularity—as a ninth-grade cheerleader. All the new activities and other stuff were just groundwork.

As spring approached once more, I practiced by the hour. I sought advice and help from the older cheerleaders. And I did everything else I could to let the coaches know how serious I was about being a cheerleader. When tryouts came I performed my routines for the judges and went home even more nervous than I had the year before.

This time my final year in junior high was at stake. If I was a nobody again in ninth grade, I would go into high school the following year as a nobody. I knew it would be even harder to escape anonymity in high school than it had been in junior high. So I told myself, *This could be my last chance.*

The next morning loudspeakers throughout the school declared the happy news. Everyone in school heard my name read as one of the next year's cheerleading squad. All my work and planning had paid off. Popularity was finally within reach.

A couple weeks after the announcement, the new cheerleaders met after school with our P.E. teacher—who was also our cheerleading sponsor—in the health classroom. There we took measurements for new skirts and sweaters and rejoiced in our good fortune at being the squad to get brand-new outfits. Then our sponsor handed out slips of paper and asked us to vote for the squad member we wanted to be our captain. When she collected the votes the rest of us headed outdoors for our first official practice.

We were standing outside the door of the gym still discussing which cheer to work on first when our sponsor walked out to join us. "Okay, girls," she said. "The captain of next year's squad is going to be Becky."

I'd never been happier in my life. In fact, happy doesn't really describe what I felt. Ecstasy was more like it. I wasn't going to be a mere cheerleader. I was *captain* of the cheerleaders. Ninth grade was going to be a great year. Guaranteed.

As I accepted the congratulations of my teammates, I especially noted Kim Calkins's reaction. She smiled her acceptance of me, but I felt certain she had to be disappointed. As the only second-year member of the squad, she must have been expecting to be chosen captain.

I smiled back at her, trying hard not to gloat—at least on the outside. Inside I couldn't help thinking, *I'm gonna be captain! I finally beat Kim at something that matters! It's really true! I'm gonna be captain!*

I was so certain that being a cheerleader would bring me the satisfaction, the accomplishment, and the popularity I'd always dreamed of that I decided to concentrate totally on my cheerleading. I'd belonged to an AAU swim team since I was eight. And that summer before ninth grade my synchronized swim team took home a seventh-place purple ribbon at the junior nationals held in Davenport, Iowa. But when that meet was over I broke the news to my swimming coach that I was giving up swimming in order to have enough time and energy for cheerleading.

Our squad practiced hard all summer. We went together to cheerleading camp. And I tried to exert my leadership through enthusiasm and hard work. I must have been working *too* hard one practice just before school started in the fall. I pulled a muscle and the doctor put me on crutches.

But I wasn't about to relinquish my leadership of the squad or my spot in the limelight. When the rest of the cheerleaders ran out on the field for the first cheer at the season's first football game, I followed as quickly as I could on my crutches. I took my appointed place in the line and stood for a moment surveying the crowd and savoring the moment. Then I shouted out the signal, "Ready! Okay!" and we launched into our first official cheer.

My injury lasted through the first three or four games. While I couldn't do cartwheels, mounts, or any of the gymnastic routines, there was nothing wrong with my mouth. Or my lungs. I could yell and cheer. I could captain the squad. And doing it all with an injury only illustrated my determination and commitment.

Cheerleading was as fun and wonderful as I'd ever dreamed. But it was also a responsibility I took very seriously. I remember one practice during basketball season. The entire squad was practicing in the hall outside the gym after school. I had the planned practice routine written out on three-by-five-inch cards so I could check off each item as we covered it.

When a couple of the girls started goofing off before we finished, I lashed into them. "The rest of us want to practice. We're working hard so we can represent our school. And I don't even think you two care." I went on to talk about the image we projected as cheerleaders, about school spirit, about how we needed to depend on each other as teammates, and more. By the time I finished my speech I was in tears. And so were the two girls. They apologized to the squad, we hugged, and practice went on.

Ninth grade went on as well. And I gloried in the spotlight. I was no longer anonymous. All the teachers in the school knew my name. All the other students knew me. I was Becky the cheerleader. Captain of the cheerleaders.

And yet I didn't feel popular. How could I? I didn't have a serious boyfriend. *Maybe next year,* I told myself, *if I can just make the high school cheerleading squad as a tenth grader. Then maybe a football player will want to date me. That would be the ultimate in popularity, the dream of dreams.*

So in April, when tryout time came around once again, I filled out my application to become a Central High School cheerleader. I knew I had a good chance. My grades were good—over 3.5 for my ninth-grade courses—and I had a year's experience behind me. I tried to write all the proper things in answer to the application essay question, "What are the responsibilities of a cheerleader—in school and out?"

> I think the responsibilities of a cheerleader, in school and out, would most of all be to represent the school in the best possible way. We should be proud to be cheerleaders and be proud of our team and school as well. I think a cheerleader should have a good attitude toward the team, no matter what the team's standings are. A cheerleader should never think a game is lost until it is all over. She should never give up and always have a positive attitude for the team she is cheering on to victory. A cheerleader should be peppy and full of spirit. A cheerleader should want to give extra time and effort to the squad and cooperate with the other cheerleaders. She should get good grades and try her best to uphold the name of the Central High School cheerleaders.

I went to all the clinics where the older cheerleaders went over the cheers, jumps, and skills required for the tryouts. I practiced like crazy, both alone and with the other members of our junior high squad who also planned to try out. And on the last Thursday afternoon in April I went to the high school gym to try out against all the ninth graders from all the other junior high schools in the district, plus tenth graders from the high school who wanted to be junior varsity cheerleaders the following year.

Almost a hundred girls sat in that huge gymnasium, all of us dressed in dark shorts, white tops, socks, and tennis shoes. And one at a time we were called up to perform a dozen required and optional skills ranging from simple jumps and cartwheels to roundoffs and back handsprings. Then we each did three cheers alone and another with a group of girls. The judges rated us on our skills and also noted personal qualities of appearance, pep, crowd appeal, poise, and posture.

And for the third year in a row I made the uneasy trek home, feeling I'd done my best yet wondering if it would be enough. I remembered the thrill and the excitement of making the squad just the year before. But I couldn't forget the terrible pain of losing in seventh grade.

At least this year I knew I wouldn't have to spend another restless night wondering and worrying. If I were selected, I'd know later that evening. It was tradition that the varsity cheerleaders would drive to the new cheerleaders' homes to give them the good news and present them with a congratulatory corsage to wear to school the next day as a victory symbol.

Of course, I was too wound up to eat supper. I couldn't even sit still. All I could do was wander nervously from one end of the house to the other, watching out the front windows for a car or pacing to the phone. While I desperately wanted to call my friends from the junior high squad to see if any of them had heard anything yet, I didn't really want to know that they'd been visited and I hadn't. *I wish someone would call me*, I thought. *But a phone call won't tell me what I want to hear. It would only mean one of my friends has no news, or bad news.* So every time I stopped and looked at the silent phone, I thought the worst and hoped for the best.

It was almost eight o'clock when a car pulled into our driveway. My heart and my stomach did a flip-flop as I saw Shawna Davis, the captain of next year's varsity cheerleaders, climb out and start up our walk. I met her at the front door, she congratulated me for making the junior varsity squad, handed me my corsage, gave me a big hug, and promised we were all "gonna have such a great year!" And then she was gone to take the good word to someone else.

I raced immediately to the phone. I hoped my friends had good news, too. But what really mattered to me was that I was going to be a high school cheerleader. The dream was coming true. And I had to tell someone before I died of excitement.

CHAPTER 2

MY SECRET WEAPON

One day early that summer between ninth and tenth grades, the high school cheerleaders held a car wash to raise money for cheerleading camp. And that event served as my introduction to the students, teachers, and parents of Central High School who drove their cars in to be washed. I had never worked harder, and I had never felt any more important, or prouder, than I did working alongside all those other cheerleaders with a pail and a sponge.

But the guys were what impressed me most that day. These weren't the junior high boys I'd been used to cheering for. These were high school football players, seventeen- and eighteen-year-old hunks who drove to the car wash in their Camaros and their TransAms just to talk with and gawk at the cheerleaders. And I was a cheerleader!

I knew exactly how Cinderella must have felt when she walked into the royal ball. I could hardly believe this was happening to me. I didn't work up enough courage that day to carry on an actual conversation with any of the football players, but that didn't keep me from looking.

And as I watched those older guys with their cars and their muscles, I told myself, *Becky, this is a whole new ball game.*

I knew I wasn't the same ugly duckling I'd been when I'd begun junior high. I'd gotten rid of the ugly glasses, finished with braces, slimmed down and filled out, let my hair grow long, and begun wearing makeup. But I'd felt unattractive for so long that I couldn't believe my looks would win me any popularity. Still somehow, amazingly, I found myself at that car wash standing in the most glorious summer sunshine sopping wet and right in the middle of the high school in-crowd.

I made up my mind right there that I would do whatever it took to stay. I even dreamed that one of those big handsome guys would become my personal prince. With all my other fantasies coming true, I began to believe it could really happen.

As the summer progressed I discovered other advantages to being a cheerleader. With my new status came instant access to an older crowd. While most of my old junior high friends still had to ask their parents for rides, members of my new circle had their own wheels. And the horizons of my life were suddenly pushed back. Way back. From seventh grade on, I had been pushing and pulling at my parents' restraints. Fights with my mom had become more frequent and more intense as my frustration with house rules also increased.

Now, just as certainly as easy access to wheels expanded my horizons, it gave me a freedom I'd never known before. I would go places without my parents' knowledge or permission. And in the process, I encountered choices I'd never had before.

Though I had never had a drink, I noticed that a lot of high school kids drank. And I was curious to find out what the big deal was. So on the Fourth of July weekend I didn't even have to think when my friend Wendy asked, "Do you wanna get some beer for tonight?"

"Sure. Let's do it. I know where we can buy it."

I'd heard other friends talk about a small ethnic grocery on the other side of town where the clerk never asked for an ID. So that's where we went early that afternoon. We walked in feeling nervous and conspicuous. Neither of us looked a bit older than our actual ages of fifteen and sixteen.

We wandered around the store for a couple of minutes, as if looking for something we couldn't find. Then when the only other customer in the place paid for her purchases and left, I picked up a six-pack and walked nonchalantly to the checkout. As I stood there wondering if the guy behind the counter would really make the sale, Wendy walked up behind me and pointed to a pack of cigarettes in the display rack. I reached for the pack, set it on the beer, and turned to wink at Wendy as the clerk rang up the purchases.

Two minutes later we were walking out the door, our illegal booty sufficiently concealed in a brown paper grocery sack. We walked home by way of the municipal park, where we were coming that night to see the city-sponsored fireworks, and stashed our beer in the bushes between the parking lot and the lake.

Droves of people trekked toward the lake as twilight was fading to darkness. When Wendy and I reached the park, I wondered for a few moments if we'd hidden the beer well enough. But as we walked from the parking area into the vast expanse of brush, where each bush looked like every other bush in the dark, I was afraid we'd hidden it too well.

I needn't have worried. The beer proved a lot easier to find than it was to drink. Right there in the sheltered undergrowth with Wendy I popped the top of my first beer. It tasted awful. *Maybe I should have bought another brand. Or maybe it's better cold,* I thought. Eventually I finished my can, and when Wendy opened her second can, so did I.

We finished off the six-pack before we came out from the bushes and joined the rest of the crowd to find a spot to sit on the grass for the coming show. By the time the first starburst exploded high in the sky above the lake, I was already experiencing a strange, yet pleasant buzzing sensation. And the exploding colors seemed especially vivid against the velvet sky.

When the grand finale faded into wisps of smoke and the people around us began gathering up lawn chairs and blankets, I very slowly maneuvered myself to my feet.

"You okay?" Wendy asked.

"Sure," I replied. And I was. I felt great.

A lot of the crowd headed for the Dairy Queen just a couple blocks away. So we walked that way, too.

As we stood in line to get waited on, a car pulled up and a boy stuck his head out of the passenger window and called to Wendy. It was John, a guy she knew from school. With him in the car were a couple of his senior buddies.

"You two wanna ride around a while?" John asked.

Wendy looked at me. When I shrugged and nodded, the doors opened. Wendy slid into the front seat with John and I climbed in the back between two guys I knew by sight but not by name.

As the driver pulled back out onto the street, the guy on my right, who introduced himself as Doug, reached down under the seat and pulled out a six-pack. "Want a beer?" he asked.

"Sure," I replied.

We cruised slowly past the park, out to the McDonald's at the edge of town and back by the Dairy Queen again. I felt a little awkward at first, sitting between two older guys I didn't really know. But after I had finished another beer I began to relax and listen and laugh along with everyone else. I seemed to fit right in.

A little while later Wendy pulled out the pack of cigarettes we'd bought that afternoon, took one for herself, and passed the rest around the car. I would have handed the pack back to Wendy but since everyone else took one, I decided I might as well.

Doug lit mine for me. I took my first puff and thought I was going to choke to death. But by taking as few and as shallow puffs as I could without being too obvious, I finished my first cigarette.

After the fifth or sixth pass of the Dairy Queen, Wendy told John we needed to be getting home since it was getting late. "I'll drop you off at your home," the driver offered.

"No," I immediately replied, "you can let us out right here."

"Right here's just fine," Wendy echoed. We both knew her parents would ask too many questions if a carload of boys dropped us off. Especially since she had told her parents we were just walking to the fireworks, stopping for something to eat, and coming right home.

The car slowed to a standstill and Doug opened his door.

But before I could climb out, he leaned over and gave me a long, hard kiss right on the mouth. I almost keeled over in surprise.

"See you around, Becky," he called as the car pulled away leaving me standing weak-kneed and trembling on the sidewalk next to Wendy. I breathlessly told her what had happened as we walked to her house. I felt like I was floating on air.

I was still too excited to sleep an hour later as I lay on the bed in Wendy's room, watching the warm summer breeze billowing the blue curtains hanging at the open window. We'd talked ourselves out, telling and retelling each other all the details of our wild and wonderful night.

Wendy was quiet now, but my mind kept racing back again and again. My first drink. My first smoke. And getting kissed by a senior boy—all in one incredible night.

Suddenly the curtains and the window began to spin and I felt very sick. I moaned and rolled over on my back to relieve the pressure on my stomach. But it didn't help. The ceiling was spinning as fast as the rest of the room. So I closed my eyes for a while and tried not to think about the gymnastics my stomach was trying to perform.

Both Wendy and I woke up the next morning feeling terribly groggy but very happy. We laughed about each other's hangovers. I decided mine was a small price to pay for the excitement I'd had the night before. I knew very well none of it would have happened if I hadn't been drinking.

The very next weekend I heard about a country-club dance in a nearby town where rumor had it there would be lots of beer. I told my folks I was going out to a movie and then spending the night at Wendy's. Instead, Wendy and I headed for the dance with some older friends who had offered to give us a ride.

Sure enough, there were kegs of beer and no one asking for IDs. The beer tasted better to me than it had the week before, and I drank more of it. We all danced for a while. John and Doug showed up, and when all the girls I came with paired off with guys later in the evening I found myself with Doug again. We danced, took a walk to the parking lot, and kissed some. When I finally climbed in the car to head home with my girlfriends, Doug waved and called out, "See you around, Hot Lips."

My carload of friends erupted with hoots and laughter, and I felt for a moment like hiding under the seat in embarrassment. But there was acceptance in the laughter I heard. And that, plus the thrill of being with Doug again, made it all worthwhile.

Those experiences the first couple of weeks in July set a pattern for every weekend that summer. I had found a social life overnight. I went out every weekend, a few times on actual dates, but usually with a carload of girlfriends. Each week I thought beer tasted better, and at every opportunity I drank enough to get me feeling good and loosened up.

Of course, these new adventures required that I begin regularly lying to my parents about where I was going and who I was going with. But lying didn't bother me because I didn't see any alternative. From the time I'd started junior high, I'd felt more and more restricted by my parents' rules. They'd said no so many times to things other kids' parents said yes to that I didn't think they were at all fair with me. Their injustice canceled out any guilt I felt about lying. The only problem I saw with lying was a practical one: I needed to be creative and fresh with the stories I told each week. And I needed to make sure my stories didn't overlap or contradict each other.

Once again, I said I was spending the night at Wendy's the evening I was asked to a rock concert in downtown Chicago by a guy who was going to be a college freshman in the fall. His name was Ben, and I'd met him through a friend. I arranged for him to pick me up a couple of blocks from home. He was right on time and we headed out of town.

As soon as we turned onto the entrance ramp of the expressway leading into the city, Ben pulled out a wrinkled looking cigarette, which I knew immediately was pot, and asked, "You ever smoked any of this?"

"No," I admitted. But not wanting to seem like little miss innocent, I added, "But I'll give it a try."

By the time we'd parked for the concert, I'd helped Ben finish off three joints. I was so wasted Ben had to prop me up just so I could walk into the concert. I don't remember one song the band played all evening, but when Ben dropped me off at Wendy's house at midnight I had a whole new adventure to tell her about.

Those few short weeks before tenth grade made my three years of junior high seem like kid's stuff. Almost as fast as a storm turns a weather vane, my life had turned and blown off in an exciting new direction. I was a different person now, with new friends and new opportunities.

The morning I was to start classes at Central High School, I felt only a tinge of the fear I'd known starting junior high. Though the high school was several times larger than Grove, I felt my identity in the school was becoming established. I was, after all, a cheerleader.

And I had discovered an invaluable secret during the summer. As drinking had become a regular weekend experience, I learned how easily it loosened me up. A few beers gave me all the courage I needed to talk and joke and laugh with the most gorgeous football players. When I drank, I never had to worry about what my older friends thought of me. Drinking made me fit in. Sometimes it even made me the life of the party.

I felt sure that drinking would be my secret weapon in capturing high school popularity.

CHAPTER 3

LIFE OF THE PARTY

I saw a lot of strangers in the halls that first day of high school, but the halls themselves were already feeling familiar. I'd been in the building several times during the summer for cheerleading practice. Just the week before school started I'd gone with all the varsity and junior varsity cheerleaders to hang banners and posters in the hallways to encourage our football team to victory in their opening game.

Since school started on a Friday, and the first varsity game of the season was scheduled for that very night, being a cheerleader solved another potential problem for me. Unlike most of my sophomore friends who'd been worrying for weeks about what they'd wear the first day of school—what would make them look good and appear older—I didn't even have a choice.

My first day outfit was my cheerleading uniform, which guaranteed my acceptance and assured me I'd be noticed even in the midst of the crowd. I walked through the halls with confidence and pride that day. I smiled and waved whenever I spotted a football player wearing a jersey. And every time one of them would smile back, the butterflies would flutter in my stomach and I'd tell myself, *High school is going to be great.*

I realized, too, that I had an advantage over a lot of other sophomores—even some of those who'd been the leaders of the in-crowd in junior high. From cheerleading and other summer activities I already knew a number of upperclassmen. I already belonged—at least more than most of my friends.

As a junior varsity cheerleader, I didn't actually cheer during the varsity games on Friday nights (the JV usually played on Saturday mornings). In many ways, I had the best of all possible worlds. I could wear my prestigious cheerleading outfit to the game, the biggest social event of the week, but I was totally free to sit in the stands, flirt with boys, drink (so long as I didn't get caught), and just have a great time.

Almost every Friday evening my friends and I would find someone to drive out to some little town in the country where I'd run into a store and buy stockpiles of lime vodka—a concoction stronger than beer, but not hard liquor (which you had to be twenty-one to buy). Then I'd head back to town and join the crowd of kids clustered in parked cars around the school parking lot. I'd drink until almost kickoff, and then join the rest of the crowd in the stands and cheer my buzzing head off. At halftime, and occasionally during time-outs, I'd slip back to the car and drink some more. By the end of the game I'd be loaded.

Some weeks, if my parents were out of town, I'd alter my routine. Instead of driving around before the game, I'd have people meet at my house—an even more private place to drink where we'd sometimes challenge each other to various drinking contests. One stunt we'd try would be to guzzle a beer. We'd tilt our head back, hold a full can of beer above our open mouth, pop it open, and gulp it down as fast as it poured out—in one giant swallow—trying not to choke or pour beer all over our clothes.

I always tried to win whatever drinking competitions we'd dream up, and I prided myself on my drinking prowess. I never minded drinking fast and hard because I never worried about getting drunk. In fact, I always drank until I was high. I liked the buzz.

The first two or three drinks relaxed me enough so I could enjoy myself; I'd never have had the nerve to do the things I did or to talk to the people I talked to if I hadn't gotten high. Five or six drinks rid me of my inhibitions, and I'd be so funny I'd get everyone laughing. The next day my friends would laugh as they recounted my antics and funny remarks again and again. "You were great last night, Becky," they'd say. "You were *sooo* funny!" And I'd bask in the glory of my life-of-the-party reputation.

I never knew how much my reputation had to do with meeting Kent. But one night as the student bus returned to the school parking lot after another away game, he offered to take some of us girls home. Kent was a senior, and while he wasn't the football star I'd always dreamed about, he was a varsity wrestler and good-looking as well.

I could hardly believe my good fortune when he dropped the other girls off before he took me home. We sat in his car and talked for a while. Kent seemed kind of shy. But when he awkwardly admitted he'd had a crush on me for some time, I immediately assured him I'd noticed him, and liked him, too. After we kissed good night, I went bouncing into the house. *Incredible,* I told myself. *A senior guy likes me. And he's so cute.* I could hardly wait to tell my friends.

In the weeks that followed, Kent and I began to date regularly. I liked him a lot. He seemed to be such a sharp guy. I couldn't figure out why he wanted to date me. And I tried not to care too much for fear he'd drop me.

Kent and I drank quite a bit when we went out together, but I drank more when I went out with the girls. Between football games, dates with Kent, and another weekly night out with the girls, my weekends filled up fast. I'd be busy Friday through Sunday night, and I'd be drinking all three nights.

It seemed most high school kids drank, but I usually drank more than most—I'd never been one to do anything halfway. My growing reputation as a big drinker simply meant I was a heartier partier and more fun to be around. The only "problem" was not being able to be too open about my drinking. I had to be careful because cheerleaders weren't allowed to drink. And I couldn't let my parents know either.

The squeaky-clean cheerleader image presented the bigger challenge. Keeping my parents in the dark merely meant that I almost always spent Friday nights at the home of some friend who had a much later curfew. All in all, I figured I had my drinking under control.

The night of the homecoming game I even turned down an invitation to a weekly pregame drinking party. I wanted to be absolutely sober because I was going to actually get to cheer; several of the varsity cheerleaders were on the homecoming court, and the JV squad had been asked to fill in. There was no way I was going to let my pregame fun interfere with my cheerleading responsibility. Plus, this was going to be my proudest cheerleading moment ever, and I wasn't about to risk losing it for a few drinks. I knew there'd be enough time to celebrate in the second half when all the ceremonies were over and the varsity squad returned to full strength.

Cheering at that homecoming game was a highlight of the football season. Where the JV squad was used to small crowds of parents and friends on Saturday mornings, the homecoming crowd was the biggest of the year. The fans were hyped up, the lights were bright. Just standing on that field at the center of all that attention was an incredible high. As we went through our routines and I listened to the response of the crowd in the stands, I told myself, *Just wait till next year. Next year I'll make varsity. Next year it'll be like this every week.*

When the homecoming ceremonies concluded at halftime and the full varsity squad returned for the third and fourth quarters, I felt a real sense of sadness to have to go back up into the stands and cheer with the rest of the crowd. But I countered the letdown with a number of trips to the parking lot, where I very quickly made up for my pregame abstinence.

In fact, I awakened the next morning a little surprised to find myself lying in my friend Sue's bed. I rolled over and looked at the shape in the sleeping bag on the floor beside the bed. Sue was still asleep. So I closed my eyes, attempting to ignore the throbbing in my head and at the same time trying to remember how I'd gotten there.

When I finally heard Sue roll over, I hung my head over the edge of the bed and asked, "You awake?"

She moaned softly in reply. "I feel like I've been dead for a week." A minute or so later she raised her head and opened her eyes just enough to squint at me. "Are you alive?"

"Barely."

"If *I* feel this horrible, I hate to think what *your* head is doing."

"What do you mean?" I asked.

Sue rolled onto her back and stared at the ceiling. "You were a riot—more smashed than I've ever seen you."

I just listened, waiting for her to go on and say something that would jog my memory. Instead, she started laughing.

"What's so funny?"

"I can't believe you turned around right there in the stands and asked Pete Gray to kiss you!"

"No! I didn't do that!"

"You certainly did!"

"I don't believe it!" Pete Gray was one of the most popular senior boys in the school. I didn't even really know him. "Are you sure? I don't remember it."

"I'm not surprised, Beck. I said you were smashed. I barely got you home."

"Why? What happened?"

"You don't remember?" She was incredulous.

"No. Tell me."

"You had a few more drinks in the parking lot after the game and you decided to walk home from school. We were cutting through the community college campus when you had to stop. You leaned up against a tree and threw up. We walked a little farther and you fell down and"—she started to laugh—"you had to crawl in the grass to a tree so you could stand up again. You threw up a couple more times and then we walked the rest of the way home.

"I don't know what made you sicker. The booze or all the laughing we did when you threw up. It was a scream!"

I didn't remember one bit of it. It was as if I hadn't even been there and Sue was telling me a story that happened to someone else. It felt a little strange when I explained to her that I didn't remember a thing after the start of the fourth quarter, but I trusted her so I didn't worry about what she thought. I just chalked the whole incident up to the fact that I'd never had that much to drink before in one night.

I had almost as much to drink that very Saturday night when I went to a big homecoming weekend party at the home of some senior guy whose parents were evidently out of town. I had a few drinks in the car so I was feeling pretty mellow by the time I arrived at the party.

It seemed like half the school was there—mostly seniors and juniors and a number of football players and cheerleaders, including Shawna Davis, the varsity squad captain. The girls I'd come with had gone their separate ways, so I just found a spot where I could lean up against the wall and watch the action and try to contemplate my good fortune. There I was, a mere sophomore, with the heart of the Central High School social scene milling around before my very eyes.

I greeted a number of familiar faces passing by. But mostly I watched, listening to the music and sipping on my supply of beer. As the evening wore on and each beer added its effect, I remember feeling as if I was slowly sliding down the wall until I sat on the floor with an empty beer can in my hand, the wall at my back, and a faceless blur of people dancing, talking, and laughing high above me. After a time of staring at moving knees and feet, I slid laboriously back up the wall and made my way to a room piled with coats. There I lay down and slept until my friends decided to head home.

I woke up the next morning with uncharacteristic regrets. I realized I'd been at one of the most prestigious parties of the year, with the most popular kids in school, and I'd spent the entire evening propped against a wall or sleeping in a spare room. I also felt bad to think that Shawna Davis had seen me so obviously drunk—not exactly the ideal image for a Central cheerleader. It was the first time since I'd begun drinking back in the summer that I felt any lingering embarrassment over my behavior. However, my regrets weren't enough to make me change my pattern of regular weekend drinking.

Somehow I continued to keep my drinking a secret from my parents. If they had any suspicions, they at least didn't confront me on the subject. There were related conflicts though.

One Sunday morning as I was trying to sleep off a hangover, my mom came into my room and stepped to the foot of my bed. "Get up, Becky," she said. "It's time to get ready for church."

I didn't respond.

"Did you hear me? Are you awake, Becky?"

"I'm awake."

"You're gonna have to hurry," she said as she retreated into the hall.

She returned a few minutes later. "Rebecca!" she exclaimed when she saw me still buried under the covers. "You're gonna be late! Get up right now!"

"I'm not going," I declared without moving.

"Yes, you are!"

"I am not!"

With each exchange the volume rose until we were yelling at each other. My father came rushing in. "Get up!" he ordered. "And stop talking to your mother like that. She's the only mother you've got." Then he turned and strode out, his role as enforcer completed.

"I can't go now," I told my mother, using my last line of defense. "There isn't even time to shower."

"Then just put your clothes on, comb your hair, and get in the car," she replied and stalked out.

Minutes later I was in the car, but my jaws were clenched and I didn't say a word the whole way to church or on the way back. And as soon as we got home again at noon, I went to my room, slammed the door, and refused to do anything with the family the rest of the day.

Every Saturday I'd try to think of some strategy that would enable me to stay home Sunday mornings. But nothing seemed to work. Although we didn't always have screaming fights about it, I always made sure my mom knew I was going against my will. Yet I never seemed to be able to wear her down.

In fact, she wasn't content with my going only to Sunday morning church. As I passed through the kitchen one Sunday afternoon, Mom asked, "Are you planning to go to youth group tonight?"

"No," was all I said. I'd gone through confirmation during ninth grade. But with all the other activities going on, I hadn't made it to youth group since school started. Besides being busy and having other priorities, I didn't want to associate with the kids in our church. Many of them were straight and didn't party, dance, or care about the things I cared about, so I didn't see any point.

But Mom refused to back off. "Why don't you think about it, Becky? When your sister was in high school she so enjoyed—"

"I'm not my sister!" I snapped. I'd heard it proudly told before that Susie had been elected president of the church youth group. She'd also been selected Outstanding Senior Girl in her class, made fantastic grades, and even won awards for good citizenship.

Any comparison with either of my siblings created additional resentments that I never voiced. I remembered how involved my parents had been in Susie's and Fred's high school experiences. Any time Susie was in any sort of program, the whole family went. I don't remember my parents ever missing one of Fred's football games; they always seemed so proud. But now that I was in high school, now that I was a cheerleader, they didn't go to my games.

I don't want to be like my sister, I told myself. *I'm my own person. And I'm not going to that youth group.*

It wasn't as if I hadn't shown some leadership of my own. Not only was I a cheerleader, but I was chosen to be a sophomore server at the school's big annual December Dance—a formal affair held for juniors and seniors. So despite a growing reputation as a big drinker and a rowdy cutup in class, I was right where I wanted to be—in the middle of the social scene. Despite my parents, I had everything under control.

One day, in health class, our P.E. instructor lectured on alcoholism. I sat in the middle of the room and joked around with my friends. The teacher talked as if we didn't know anything about alcohol, so we feigned surprise at everything she said. "Wow." "No kidding?" "Is that right?"

When she listed some of the warning signs of a drinking problem, we all pretended to furiously take notes. The whole time we were rolling our eyes, making faces at each other, and snickering under our breaths.

I did take notice when she wrote, "Blackouts—loss of memory," on the board. Staring at those words for a few moments, I thought of the night of the homecoming game. But I shrugged that off as the teacher also wrote, "Frequent absences from work, drinking in the morning, drinking every day, and drinking alone."

None of those signs described me. I didn't need to drink. I just did it for the fun and the excitement. Nothing more. I knew some people had drinking problems; I'd seen derelicts on the sidewalk in downtown Chicago, but drinking wasn't a problem for me. If anything, it was an advantage.

CHAPTER 4

TROUBLE HITS

*B*efore long, problems did develop. Lots of them.

One night when my folks were to be gone, a friend named Penny and I worked out a plan. About a half hour after my parents left, she and our two boyfriends arrived. We turned up the stereo and turned down the lights. The guys poured some shots and beers, and while I'd never tried that combination before, I gamely downed two or three rounds. Then Kent and I claimed the living room couch and began making out.

We'd hardly begun to warm up when I heard a sound that chilled me to the depths of my soul. A key turned in the lock, the front door swung open, and my father stepped into the house.

I froze momentarily in Kent's arms. But my dad stopped in the semidarkness not five feet from the couch where we were lying and nonchalantly began to light his pipe. He hadn't seen anything or anyone yet. But I knew he would.

When I saw him reach for the light switch, I leaped from the couch. And by the time the lights came on I stood in the middle of the room, screaming at my father. "What are you doing here? You said you were going to be gone for the evening!"

I watched as the shock and total surprise on his face changed almost instantly to puzzlement then to anger as he glanced quickly around the room and sized up the situation.

"What's going on here?" he bellowed back at me. But he knew.

He stuck his head out the front door to call to my mother

who was sitting in the car with another couple waiting for Dad to retrieve whatever it was he'd returned for. "Joan," he yelled, "you'd better get in here!"

So Mom hurried in, took a quick look around, and immediately added to the anger and hysteria. Right away my parents sent my friends packing out the front door. And that set me off on a giant tirade. "Now look what you've done. You've humiliated me. You've ruined everything." And on and on.

In the shouting match that ensued my parents said some very harsh things. And I felt as if all the arguments of the past three years, all the times my parents had told me no, had built up and built up until there was a volcano of resentment inside me that was ready to erupt. I exploded at my parents, screaming that I hated them and threatening to run away. And as they reeled from my blast, I fled to my room. When my parents eventually went out to the car to join their curious, waiting friends, I did run away to Penny's where the guys met us. And we had a party anyway.

But my secret was finally out. I didn't have to pretend anymore. That blowup drove a wedge between me and my parents and communication wasn't the same again. When we weren't arguing about my drinking, there always seemed to be something else to fight about.

Mom would criticize my choice of clothes, or they'd demand to know where I was going, with whom, when I'd be back, and we'd all be screaming at the top of our lungs. We'd fight about how much money they had to give me to spend on a Friday night, or they'd tell me I couldn't stay over at a friend's house and I'd do it anyway. I felt they were so restrictive that I challenged every decision until home became more of a war zone than a refuge.

I thought a lot about running away. And I threatened to on numerous occasions.

The escalating conflicts at home made school seem like another hassle. Some teachers seemed to have as many demands as my parents, so I started pushing the limits just to let them know I didn't need them either. That I'd do whatever I wanted, whenever I wanted.

Almost every day in almost every class I'd ask for a pass to go to the bathroom. I could read the disbelief in teachers' eyes when I insisted I needed to leave. But they knew and I knew they didn't really have a choice. I always got the pass. And I'd use the opportunity to socialize in the hallways on the way to and from the bathroom before sauntering back to class in my own sweet time.

Homework was another unpleasant hassle. I'd do it if I felt like it. And when I didn't, I had one of the biggest repertoires of excuses in the history of high school. My fast talking could get me out of almost as many predicaments as it got me into. Almost.

I'd earned a reputation during junior high for being a mouthy smart aleck. And my conduct marks after the first nine weeks of my sophomore year guaranteed I wouldn't be inheriting my sister's citizenship awards. I was called down for talking in class more times than you could count on a pocket calculator. And I made numerous trips to the office for talking back when teachers seemed pushy or unfair.

My typing teacher was the biggest pain. Miss Klooney was a young, new teacher and very demanding. I didn't like her and let her know it. I'd give her dirty looks while she was talking to the class, and I'd toss my papers down on her desk instead of handing them to her. One day after the bell rang, as we were all filing out of the room I turned and said to one of my friends, loud enough for Miss Klooney to hear, "I hate that lady."

My grades depended to a large extent on my attitude toward my teachers. If my relationship with a teacher was good, my grades were good. But when a teacher rubbed me the wrong way, I wouldn't do the work. As a result my grades dropped from a nearly straight-A average of 3.8 in junior high, to about a 3.0 for the first semester in high school.

The only reason my grades stayed as high as they did was my habitual practice of cheating. I'd copy somebody's homework in almost every class. For Spanish quizzes I'd write the verb conjugations on the palm of my hand. Before one big Spanish test I wrote an entire essay in the gutter margin of my English-Spanish dictionary, which we were allowed to have on our desks.

However, the easiest course to cheat in proved to be Algebra I. The teacher, Mr. Fitzgerald, was almost retirement age and in very poor health. When he wasn't lecturing, he would just sit at his desk while we worked problems. Often he would fall asleep. So algebra tests were a cinch; students would pull out their books for easy reference or merely exchange answers or papers with friends sitting next to them. I made easy A's without having to learn a thing.

The problem came when Mr. Fitzgerald decided to retire after the first semester and was replaced by a young teacher. The new man not only expected us to know some basic algebra, but stayed awake in class and was sharp enough to spot cheating a mile away. I hated him right away and promptly decided to drop algebra and transfer to an easier math class for the second semester.

That's how I ended up with Mr. Cottel. He was the epitome of the kind of person we called a "Poindexter." Tall. Gangly. Mid-twenties. Black horn-rimmed glasses were the most fashionable thing he ever wore. You'd see him in the hallway making a beeline for his classroom, leaning forward about forty degrees and carrying a tattered briefcase. He talked in a high, scratchy voice and had a loud laugh that punctuated his conversations and lectures at strange and unexpected points. In other words, he was a real nerd and the butt of a lot of laughter.

As you'd expect, he didn't get a lot of respect in his classes. You could tell it bothered him and that made him a vulnerable, hard-to-resist target of fun. One day, not long after I had joined his class, I was turned completely around in my seat talking to the guy behind me, when Cottel said, "Please be quiet, Becky."

I whirled around. "I wasn't doin' nuthin'," I responded indignantly. Some of my classmates grinned.

"You were turned around and talking."

"You must be seeing things," I said, and someone laughed.

"Don't get smart with me, young lady."

"Then stop picking on me, you jerk." With that a number of students egged me on.

"That's it!" Cottel declared. "You're going to the office." And he took my arm as if he were going to lead me to the door. I jerked away from him and snapped, "Don't you touch me."

"Then get out of here, right now," he shouted.

I told him I would go when I got good and ready, and he repeated his order. Right in the middle of our fight one of the other kids in the class walked up to Cottel, whipped out a pair of scissors, and cut six inches off the bottom of his tie. It was no great loss. Everyone in the whole school joked about Cottel's ties—they were the oldest and ugliest I'd ever seen. But that was the end of the argument right then and there. The man was so furious that I fled the room without another word and made the trek to the office along with my scissor-wielding cohort. By the time we stood in front of the principal to explain our behavior I had formulated a heartfelt defense for our actions. "That man has no business being a teacher," I argued. "How do you expect us to respect someone like that? He can't even control a class, let alone teach."

I received a Saturday suspension as a result of that little incident. But I didn't mind because half the school was talking about it for a week. I loved the attention, the way people turned to look at me in the hall, the way people who'd never spoken to me before would grin and say, "Hi, Becky."

So in effect, I had gotten away with it. I almost always knew just how far I could push things. And in doing so, I was showing everyone that I didn't have to care about teachers or grades to have what I wanted. I was a cheerleader, and was careful to keep my grades high enough and not get into any trouble serious enough to jeopardize that.

That's why I was caught completely by surprise one Thursday afternoon, just a day before the biggest basketball weekend of the season, when the cheerleading coach pulled me off to the side at the start of practice to say, "I just got a progress report on you from the office. You're not going to be able to cheer this week."

"Progress report?" I couldn't imagine why. "What class?"

"Typing."

"No way," I said. "I made a C in there last semester."

The coach shrugged. "According to the progress report Miss Klooney sent to the office, you're not passing that course. I'm sorry, but you'll have to sit out until you get your grade back up."

"I'll see about that," I declared as I spun on my heel and stalked off for the typing room on the second floor. School had been out only a few minutes and I thought I might catch Miss Klooney still in her room.

She looked up from her desk when I stormed in demanding to know, "What are you doing to me? I don't have a problem in typing. How could you send down a progress report on me?"

Her voice remained maddeningly calm as she said, "You got a D on the test we had Monday."

"You're kidding. That was just a quiz. You give those almost every week."

"Yes," she said, "but that's the only grade you have for this new semester. So until you bring that grade up, you've got a D in typing. And I was required to send in a progress report."

"You're telling me I'm off the cheerleading squad because of one stupid little typing test?" I felt certain she was enjoying this revenge.

"I'm sorry," she said. But I didn't believe her.

I had too much pride to beg. So I turned and stormed out of the classroom, slamming the door as I went.

I was still so furious the next night that I drank an entire quart of Boone's Farm apple wine before the game. When I walked into the gymnasium and took a seat up in the stands, I was bombed. While my teammates led the crowd in cheers, I sat in the stands and made critical remarks about the opposing cheerleaders. And at halftime I made my way around the end of the floor and headed for the concession stand on the visitors' side of the gym.

Some of the opposing cheerleaders had been rival cheerleaders in junior high school, so they knew me. And one of them rather snootily asked, "What did you do that you can't cheer tonight, Becky?"

I called her a dirty name. She said something similar to me and I clenched my fists and started for her. One of my cheerleading teammates grabbed me from behind and dragged me out the door before the whole thing exploded.

When I woke up the next morning and remembered the incident I worried about the possible disciplinary implications. Initially I also felt embarrassed, but that feeling quickly changed to deeper hatred toward my typing teacher for creating the problem in the first place. I told myself, *She probably gave that quiz just to get me. And I'll never forgive her for it.*

I wasn't disciplined for trying to pick a fight at the game; I was never even sure the cheerleading coach heard what happened. But the incident did create the first open conflict between me and some of the other cheerleaders who had witnessed or heard about the little scene.

The captain of the JV squad and another girl, both juniors, had been mortified by my behavior at the game. They came to me afterward to say they were concerned about the image of the squad because of the incident and also because of my reputation as a big drinker. But I made it extremely clear to them that my life was my business and none of theirs.

Partly out of spite toward those girls, I brought some beer to school one morning. I skipped first period with a couple of guys from my first hour class to go out and sit in the parking lot in a friend's van and get loaded. Then I went to class for the rest of the morning. But I didn't do it all for spite. Part of me was simply curious to see what it was like to go to school high. I got a few funny looks in some of my classes, but nobody said anything. Even though I got away with it, and doing it gave me a rush—kind of a high-risk experience—I decided I wouldn't do it again.

Before the end of the basketball season, I would, however, cache a bottle of wine in my locker before every home game. Right after the JV game I would sneak back to my locker and drink until I would get a good buzz. Then I would go back to the gym for the varsity game, sit in the stands, and cheer with the rest of the crowd. And though I never got caught doing that either, it was becoming more and more obvious to people around me that I was taking fewer and fewer precautions.

Once, almost at the end of basketball season, some of us cut last-period study hall, snuck out to my friend's van in the parking lot, and I got blasted. The final bell rang, students streamed out of the building onto the buses, my friends took off for home, and I headed back inside for cheerleading practice.

I was drunk as a skunk and almost passed out on one of the mats before practice started. I thought it was so funny I could barely contain myself.

My coach didn't see anything funny. She angrily ordered me to go home and sober up. She didn't turn me in or kick me off the team, but that incident added one more level to the growing wall of resentment between the coach, the rest of the team, and me. What really ticked me off was the way they kept trying to force me into a goody-goody mold; they just wouldn't accept me the way I was.

There was really only one time when I got angry with myself for a drinking-related problem. One weekend when I had partied hard for three straight nights, I felt too hung over to face school on Monday morning. It wasn't the first Monday I'd missed so I didn't think anything about it until I was walking to homeroom Tuesday morning.

The JV squad captain stopped me in the hall. "Where were you yesterday, Becky?" she asked. "You missed program pictures."

"What?"

"The cheerleading squads had group pictures taken for

the game programs yesterday. Everyone was there except you." I didn't think I was imagining the smugness in her voice. "Were you sick?"

"Yeah. I was sick," I said. But I certainly hadn't been as sick as I felt right then as the crushing truth sank in. *I missed pictures. When everyone gets their program at the game, my picture isn't going to be with the rest of the cheerleaders.* I was hurt.

By the time the hurt festered through homeroom period, I was angry. When I spotted another one of the cheerleaders in the hall I wanted to know, "Why didn't you call me? Why didn't anyone remind me that pictures were yesterday?" I would have crawled to school if necessary for pictures; all I'd had was a hangover. But mostly I was angry at myself for messing up, for losing out on the recognition I'd worked so hard to earn. I couldn't believe I had forgotten something so important. And the most sickening thing was the realization that it was too late then to do anything about it.

But something else happened early that spring that was completely out of my control—something that made picture day pale by comparison. The phone rang one morning just before Mom left for work, while I was still getting dressed for school. Someone from my dad's office was calling to tell us Dad had just collapsed and was on his way to the hospital in an ambulance.

A half hour later we sat in a hospital waiting room, waiting for some word. Finally a doctor came out of the emergency room and began telling Mom that it looked like Dad had suffered a massive stroke. He said it was too early to tell how he'd come out of it, or even if he would come out of it at all.

As the doctor tried to answer Mom's questions and the seriousness of it all sank in, I reached into my purse and pulled out a cigarette. I had lit it and taken a long drag before I looked up and noticed my mother's surprised, disapproving glare. *She had to learn I smoked sooner or later,* I told myself. *And she's not going to make a scene here. There's Dad to worry about.*

I was right. Even after the doctor left, Mom didn't say a thing about my cigarette. Or the rest of the pack I smoked as we waited for some new word.

The waiting room scene seemed like something out of a strange foreign movie with no subtitles. New characters filed in and out talking among themselves, but everyone seemed part of a different drama. Even my mother and I seemed in separate worlds. And none of it made any sense or seemed to have any reason.

The one fact I knew was true—that my father might die—didn't make any sense either. How could he die? Why?

Oh God! I prayed. *If you'll just let my dad live, I'll do anything you want.* I'd had so many conflicts with my father that I considered him a "no" man, someone who always seemed to say no to everything that mattered to me. I hadn't felt particularly close to him in years, but I certainly didn't want him to die.

Despite my desperate prayer, the next word we received wasn't much better. He'd stabilized, but he wasn't responding. He couldn't talk and there was no movement in any of his limbs. It was entirely possible that even if he lived, he might be a vegetable. The only answer to any question was, "We'll have to wait and see."

Four or five days later, Dad did begin to talk again. Incredibly, in time, he began to move and then to walk. Eventually everything came back to him but some of his memory. He had occasional seizures, but after a few weeks of therapy he was ready to leave the hospital and finish recuperating at home.

When the hospital released Dad, the doctor told my mom and me that we couldn't allow him to lose his temper or get his blood pressure worked up or he might suffer another stroke. And that could be fatal.

So the atmosphere at home changed drastically. Mom and I worked out an unspoken truce. We would discontinue any fight the moment Dad walked into the room. We never screamed like we had before, at least not when Dad was home. I continued to resent her demands and restrictions, and she resented my lack of respect and failure to live up to her expectations. I suspected she held me at least partially responsible for adding to the stress that caused Dad's stroke. And sometimes I wondered about that myself. It wasn't anything we ever verbalized or anything I could change; I can't say I felt any guilt over it. So other than the volume of our fights, nothing else about our relationship really changed.

I drank just as much as ever and lied just as often to cover myself. My mom never did make an issue of my smoking except to forbid me from smoking in the house. So when I needed a cigarette I'd go in the bathroom, lock the door, open the window, and try to blow all my smoke outside. Sometimes when I'd come out my mother would confront me.

"Were you smoking in there?"

"No," I'd lie. Maybe since we both knew better, I didn't feel any guilt about that either.

With Dad's stroke and recovery, those spring weeks seemed to fly by. Suddenly it was nearly time for next year's cheerleading tryouts.

I'd heard rumors the year before that I'd had the highest scores on the JV squad—higher even than a couple of the older girls who'd made the varsity. So I didn't have any doubts that I had the athletic skill to make the team. All my friends seemed to assume I was a cinch to make the varsity squad as one of the junior members. But with my past conflicts and problems, I wasn't so sure I'd be picked—even if my scores were high enough.

The more I worried about not making it, the more I could see it happening. I didn't know if I could take that kind of humiliation. *They want to make me into some kind of Suzie Straitlace, and they don't like me because they know they can't do it,* I told myself. *I don't need that kind of aggravation.*

When I told my friends I was thinking about not trying out for cheerleading next year no one believed me. Their response sealed my decision. They acted as if I didn't have any choice, as if I needed to be a cheerleader. So I determined to show them.

I don't think anyone seriously believed I'd dump cheerleading until the first day of mandatory clinics. If you didn't go to the first clinic, you couldn't try out.

I didn't go.

I did, however, hang around the building for a while after school. And I wandered down to the gym, where I stood in the shadows outside an open door and watched for a few minutes as the senior cheerleaders went through the routines the aspiring cheerleaders were expected to do during tryouts.

They probably wonder why I'm not in there. But they're probably all secretly glad because it means one more available spot on the team.

I could make it if I wanted to, I assured myself, *if I cared enough to live by their rules. They all know that. But I don't care anymore. And now they'll all know that, too. I don't need them or cheerleading anymore.*

I watched a while longer before I turned and walked down the darkened hall. The bitterness didn't completely fill the emptiness inside where I'd always kept my dreams.

Getting drunk that night didn't help much either.

CHAPTER 5

FIGHTING FOR CONTROL

My decision to drop out of cheerleading pretty much cut me off from the jock crowd. So I spent most of my time looking for a new crowd.

That's why every Thursday night I'd go to a pizza pub that had dancing. That was where I met Trish, Alex, Ben, and a whole bunch of kids from neighboring Arlington High School. Friday nights I'd go with the Arlington crowd to a ski resort where there was a bar and a live band. Saturday night I'd go wherever the action was, such as a party at somebody's house. And on Sundays I'd just drive around and drink.

Almost all the kids in my new crowd were at least a year older than I. Some had lots of money and the things it could buy—nice clothes and fast cars. Being only sixteen, with not much money, I had to earn my membership in the group in other ways. Like drinking more and laughing louder than anyone else.

I'd just gotten my license, so I usually volunteered to drive. Somehow I always got everyone home safely, even though I was drinking a six-pack or more almost every night we went out.

As many as three or four nights a week I would arrange to stay at a friend's—someone whose parents wouldn't be up to smell the beer on me. But my own parents knew I was drinking—and drinking a lot. The times I would go home I would be so late and in such bad shape my parents didn't know what to do with me.

The fragile truce Mom and I had forged when Dad came home from the hospital was broken by June. She lectured, yelled, and cried, but nothing she did changed anything—except maybe Dad's blood pressure. The worst battles took place between Mom and me. But Dad still knew about them.

The first time my mom threatened to have me committed to the local juvenile detention center, I just laughed. "For what?"

"For being incorrigible," she said.

I saw she was serious, but I laughed again. "Just try it!"

She said she would, but as many times as she threatened that summer, she didn't. I never really worried about the possibility.

On several occasions, usually in the middle of a disagreement, she'd insist that I would at least have to go for some counseling. "As soon as we can get an appointment."

I would scream, argue, and refuse to even consider it. "I'm not the one with the problems. You are!"

As I walked to the door one muggy summer evening, my mom stopped me. She wanted to know where I was going and when I'd be back. "I don't know," I retorted. "And I wouldn't tell you if I did."

"You'd better be back before midnight," she warned.

I couldn't let those words go unchallenged. "I will if I feel like it," I snapped, and the conversation went rapidly downhill from there.

She said I had better do as she said. I told her she couldn't make me. And as we began shouting back and forth, weeks and months of pent-up frustration poured out of my mother. As her anger climbed to a level I had never seen before, she accused me of disgracing the family and threatening my father with another stroke. She said if I wanted to stay under their roof, I had better start abiding by their rules. "If you don't," she concluded, "you can get out!"

"Fine!" I told her. "I'll leave!" I stomped off to my room, pulled a suitcase out of my closet, and started filling it with clothes.

Moments later Mom charged into the room. "What do you think you're doing?"

"I'm leaving. You gave me a choice. And I choose to leave!"

"You're not leaving this house!"

"Just watch me!" I folded another pair of jeans and put them into my suitcase.

"You're not going anywhere!" She grabbed the pants and threw them on the floor. I picked them up and very deliberately put them back. Then she grabbed a whole stack of clothes from my suitcase and flung them across the room as she screamed again that I wasn't going anywhere.

I screamed right back. "I hate you and you can't stop me." The whole time we were screaming at each other I was trying to understand the irony of it all: My mom tells me to shape up or ship out, and then she won't let me leave! The obvious irrationality only fueled my feelings that I was a victim of injustice.

Half the clothes I owned were strewn around the room by the time my father came rushing in to see what all the ruckus was about. Outnumbered, and still stinging from my mom's accusations about my effect on Dad, I quit the fight and let my father put my suitcase away.

But later, when my parents went to their own room, I quickly packed and left. For three days I stayed at my friend Penny's house until my parents finally found me and begged me to come home.

I agreed to give it another try. It was only a matter of days before we were at each other again. And again. And again. Several times that summer I packed a bag or a suitcase and slipped out my bedroom window during the night and went to Penny's. Her mom would always make me call home the next morning to let my parents know where I was. But I wanted to scare them and to let them know I would make my own decisions.

The atmosphere at Penny's house was such a contrast to my home that it sometimes added to my frustration. Her parents seemed so warm and friendly. Their family went out to eat together and took special vacation trips. I remember one time when Penny plopped down on her dad's lap and gave him a big hug and he held her for a while like a little girl as they laughed and talked. I thought, *I don't ever remember my dad holding me on his lap like that.* And I wished he would. I wished we could somehow be a happy family, but wishing didn't make it so.

By the time August rolled around and another school year approached, we all were weary of the constant confrontations. I knew I wasn't going to give in, and I didn't expect my parents to make any drastic changes in their attitudes either. So I started thinking about some way out.

The idea that came to me seemed the only viable alternative. I decided to check out the feasibility of graduating from high school a year early.

When I suggested the option to my mom, I was a little surprised at her willingness to consider the idea. I think we both felt we couldn't go on living as we were for two more years of high school—one year, maybe. At least we'd have an end in sight; I could head off for college in another twelve months.

From my perspective, there was less and less reason to stay in high school. I wasn't going to be in cheerleading, and I was spending most of my time with senior friends anyway. All in all, high school was turning out to be a real drag. So why not get it over with as soon as possible?

Mom and I sat together across the desk from the guidance counselor, waiting as the women leafed through my file. The verdict came down positive. "If we drop Becky's elective and her study hall, it looks like we can fit in her senior requirements. As long as she can keep her grades up, she should be able to graduate next spring."

The very next week I walked into Central High School to start my senior year. But what a year.

The wild pattern of summer hardly slowed down. Where other years I had always been careful not to jeopardize my cheerleading role, this year partying had replaced popularity as the driving force in my school life.

Now I went to the Friday night football games only to drink and see who was with whom. Sometimes as the cheerleaders worked through a familiar routine I'd remember what it was like to stand in the lights and try to stir up the crowd. Then I'd tell myself, *I could be down there if I wanted to be. But I don't. I'm doing what I want and the rest of them can't hassle me anymore.*

But as the first weeks of school passed, I realized I did miss the camaraderie and the excitement of cheerleading. So when the announcement came out saying it was time for wrestling cheerleader tryouts, I swallowed my pride and tried out. Wrestling cheerleading wasn't that prestigious—only parents and girlfriends even attended the matches. But the positive side of that was that the cheerleading coach required very little of the squad; she hardly ever went to a match and only occasionally attended the practices. We'd be pretty much on our own, so we could have all the fun we wanted with none of the hassles.

I almost walked out and scrapped my whole plan when I found out the varsity cheerleader in charge of the tryouts was someone who'd given me a real hard time the year before. I almost walked out again when she pulled me aside and told me I wouldn't even be considered for the cheerleading squad if I was going to create the same kind of problems I had the year before. It was an obvious threat, an attempt on her part to let me know she had some say-so over me. I stifled the urge to tell her what I thought of her and promised to be a model cheerleader if selected—partly because I wanted to do it, but mostly because I wasn't going to give this girl the satisfaction of seeing me quit.

Eight seniors made the squad. Four of us already hung around together on a regular basis. So my plan had worked. We were going to have a blast! We weren't as prestigious as the football/basketball cheerleaders, so we were in it just to have fun.

And we did.

The wrestling coach, Mr. Rioni, had some responsibility for the cheerleaders. He was a fairly funny teacher. For example, I had a new boyfriend, another wrestler named Kent. Once, on the bus heading to a match at another school, I climbed onto Kent's lap, planted a long passionate kiss on his lips, and then gave him a big hickey on his neck. Everybody laughed about it, including Mr. Rioni.

En route to another match, we stopped to eat at a McDonald's. Afterward I carried my half-finished Coke onto the bus and laced it with gin from a fifth I'd stashed away earlier. I had heard that you couldn't smell gin on a person's breath. No one ever said anything about my being loaded that day, although I almost lost it during one of the cheers and I thought for sure I was in trouble.

I did get in trouble at one match—an afternoon affair in the high school gym of a neighboring suburb. I stood in front of the mirror in the girl's bathroom, adjusting my cheerleading sweater and taking the last couple of drags on a cigarette when a stern-looking, middle-aged woman walked in. She stopped just inside the door, sniffed the air, looked at the cigarette in my hand, and with an air of authority marched right up to me. I didn't know she was the dean.

"Come with me," she ordered. Taking my arm, she led me out of the bathroom and down the hall to the gym. The wrestling teams were doing warm-ups as she directed me over to Mr. Rioni and announced: "I found this cheerleader smoking in the rest room." The tone of her voice was saying, *What are you going to do about that?*

I could see the color rising in Mr. Rioni's neck. I'd embarrassed him in front of an administrator of another school and he was ticked. He clamped his big meaty hand on the back of my neck and said, "You're in big trouble, young lady. And if you don't straighten out fast, you're gonna be in bigger trouble."

I happened to have Mr. Rioni for government class, so when I walked into his room the next day, he called me to the front of the class. "Let me have your purse, Becky."

"What for?" I wanted to know.

"Just hand it here."

"Why?"

He didn't answer. He just snatched it out of my grip and dumped the contents on his desk. Then he picked out my nearly full pack of menthol cigarettes, ripped them open, and ceremoniously dropped them into the trash can as everybody else in the room looked on, laughing.

Now I was mad. But instead of showing it, I just laughed, stuffed everything back into my purse, and walked to my seat. The next time I went to class he did the same thing. And the time after that. I began tossing my cigarettes in my locker every day just before government. When I forgot, he'd grin victoriously and destroy my cigarettes. Checking my purse became a daily ritual that entertained my classmates and spawned something of a love/hate relationship between Mr. Rioni and me.

Yet somehow, I always seemed to avoid any serious trouble.

Like the night Trish, Alex, and Ben picked me up after a home wrestling match. As we all piled into Ben's Camaro after the match, I saw the case of Coors stashed on the floor of the backseat and knew we had everything we needed.

We cruised around for a while until Trish got giggly high and said, "I have to go to the john."

So Ben laughed and pulled off the side of the road and onto the grass of the local cemetery. Trish opened the door, ran twenty or thirty yards back into the cemetery, and stepped behind a tree as we all laughed at her.

Just as she came running back and jumped into the car, a spotlight hit us. A police car pulled up from behind and the officer got out. It was too late to ditch the beer; we were caught red-handed.

When he shone his flashlight around the inside of the car, the officer recognized our driver. "What are *you* doing out here, Ben?"

"Just heading home from a wrestling match over at Central," Ben told him.

"You've got two problems here," the policeman told him. "You've got open beer in the back and you've got minors out after curfew. I think you'd better take these girls home and go home yourself, or you may get into trouble."

"Okay, I'll do that," Ben responded. "Thanks for the warning."

As we pulled back out onto the highway, I let out a big sigh of relief and we all burst into laughter. It pays to ride with the son of Arlington's mayor.

Instead of going directly home, we drove across the town line into the adjoining town, where Ben pulled into a dark alley behind a grocery store and stopped the car. We were drinking and making out when another spotlight swept over the car. One of the town's finest policemen climbed out of his car to check us out. He also knew the major's son, so he simply told us to get along home. We promised we would, and we headed back into Arlington to find another place to park.

No sooner had we found a dark corner of a shopping center parking lot than another police car pulled up. It was the same officer who'd run us out of the cemetery, and when he saw who we were, he chewed us out and told us he was going to follow us home.

So our evening ended earlier than we'd planned. But we all went home with a hilarious tale to tell our friends the next day, about how we got caught drinking by the cops three times in one night and were still able to get away with it.

Although I avoided serious trouble with authorities that year, my partying pattern didn't come without a price. It cost me several relationships. Especially with my junior friends. They never did understand my decision to graduate a year early. I still had a couple of classes with them, but I was taking senior courses, too. We just didn't share as much of our lives as we had before.

A contributing factor was that my new Arlington friends, being a year older, could get into bars. A couple of them were eighteen and legal. So I manufactured a fake ID card. It wasn't hard. I turned seventeen in December anyway. So all I had to do was get a good copy of my birth certificate, white out the last digit of my birth year, type in a three instead of a four, and make one final copy that looked perfectly legitimate.

I found a lot more action—dancing and guys—in the bars than you could find just cruising around. So as time passed, I found fewer nights to spend with my old friends.

Then came a night when I canceled my plans with some of my old friends at the last minute, claiming I didn't feel well. The real reason was that Trish and I had decided to check out a new bar. When my old friends found out the truth a couple days later, I endured a week's worth of dirty looks and sullen silences. We made up later, but our relationships were never the same after that.

I felt bad about the rift between us. We'd all been good friends for a long time and I still wanted to be friends, but other things were crowding out our friendships. Our relationships dwindled rapidly.

I had some similar misunderstandings with Kent. He was a little younger than I was, too. He didn't want to take the risk of going to bars, and he didn't like me going without him. We continued to date into the winter; we'd go out pretty regularly and have a good time. But we kept having fights about my nights out with the girls. I'd have to say ours was an on-and-off, hot-and-cold relationship.

He could be so sweet. On Valentine's Day evening he picked me up. We drove only a couple of blocks from my house before he pulled into a parking lot, stopped the car, reached into the backseat, and presented me with a dozen long-stemmed red roses. A warm romantic sensation filled me and I thought, "So this is what it feels like to be loved—to be in love."

The next night when I wanted to go to a dance bar with Trish and another Arlington girl, Kent and I had a big fight and broke up again. It was like that the rest of my senior year. We'd go out for a couple of weeks, then we'd fight and break up for a week. I liked Kent a lot, but I wasn't going to let him keep me away from my partying.

Going to bars had exposed me to a wide range of hard liquor. I could get higher faster than I ever had drinking beer. I still drank beer, but even when I went out cruising with friends, I'd usually take something stronger. I drank a lot of what we called Mad-Dog—MD 20:20, a potent Mogen-David wine with more than a 20 percent alcohol content. A pint of that a night hit me like a six-pack high without the bloated feeling. The only drawback, and it seemed pretty insignificant, was that there were more and more mornings when I couldn't recall everything that had happened the night before.

I also did a lot of pot. Its more mellow high gave me warm feelings of closeness to my friends. I hardly ever bought any. Yet I always seemed to be able to get dope whenever I wanted it.

But lots of high schoolers experimented with more than just beer and pot. Word always spread about those who did hard drugs or had "loose" reputations. So I still had reservations about those things. My reasons weren't particularly moral ones: The drugs scared me, and sex was something I felt needed to wait until I discovered my true love. In a way, my abstinence in both areas was a way of proving to myself that I was still in control of my life.

And control was becoming increasingly important to me. Maybe because so many things about my senior year weren't turning out like they always had in my dreams.

CHAPTER 6

A NEW START

One of the ways I decided to exert more control in my life was financial. Asking my folks for money every time I went out was growing old, not to mention the number of times doing so would start a major argument. I'd scrounge all the loose change I could find in the house, but I could never swipe too much at a time off my dad's dresser without getting caught. So I never seemed to have as much as I wanted.

The resulting financial frustration was the main motivation to look for a job after wrestling season concluded. It didn't take long to land a Saturday waitressing job at a local Denny's franchise. The job proved tedious. And on the days I opened up the restaurant at 6:00 A.M. after a wild Friday night of drinking, I doubted whether any amount of money was worth it. The hours were too long, the customers often ungrateful. I decided after the first few weeks that I would never choose any career related to the restaurant business. The only reason I didn't quit was Penny. She worked with me, sharing in the pain as well as in the rewards.

Every Saturday afternoon we went out and celebrated the end of another shift. The two of us would go have a few drinks at Wine and Roses, a seedy motorcycle bar next to the railroad tracks on the tough side of town. The place always had music, dancing, and no end of unusual people. We'd sit on stools at the bar, complaining about our customers or our tired feet, drinking mugs of beer until I'd spent all my tip money, feeling sophisticated and very independent.

While my part-time job at least provided the satisfaction of a regular paycheck, my full-time role as a graduating high school senior turned out to be something of a letdown.

Senior prom proved a major disappointment. Technically, I was classed as a graduating junior, so there was some question at first whether or not I could go. When I pointed out that I would never have another prom, I was granted special permission to attend. But since my boyfriend, Kent, was just a junior, I had to be the one to invite him. To make matters worse, we had another big fight the week before prom and out of spite I invited his best friend, another junior. So instead of the romantic milestone I'd always dreamed of—a fantasy evening spent dancing with a prince charming who'd chosen me above everyone else in the kingdom—I spent a rather dull evening making small talk with my ex-boyfriend's friend.

I had a more memorable time the very next week during finals. Or rather *in between* finals. Seniors had two tests scheduled per day—the first from nine to eleven in the morning and the second from one to three in the afternoon. After the morning exam, I talked a couple of my friends into going with me to Wine and Roses for lunch. We ordered a round of greasy-spoon burgers and fries, plus a pitcher of beer to share. And we laughed at our daring adventure of eating our last high school lunch together in a bar and drinking beer before our last final. Before we knew it, the Budweiser clock behind the bar said 12:45 and we'd finished off three pitchers of beer.

I walked into my chemistry final seven minutes late. Everyone else was already hunched over their papers, pencils scratching away furiously.

"You're late," Mrs. Goldsmith said, motioning me to follow her into the enclosed office in the back of the room, between the classroom and the chemistry lab. She handed me the test, gave me the verbal instructions, and explained that I'd have only five extra minutes to complete the exam when everyone else finished. And then she stepped back into the classroom, closing the door behind her.

I couldn't believe my luck. Earlier I'd managed to acquire a copy of the test, with the answers. I'd been trying to figure out how to check it during the exam to make sure my answers were right. Now with a private office all to myself, I had only to pull the completed test out of my purse and quickly copy the answers onto my own paper. I finished so early I decided I'd better sit and wait a more realistic amount of time. An eternity passed and I looked out the office window to see everyone else still poring over their exams. I decided, *What the heck? I'm graduating next week anyway;* walked quickly to the front of the room, put my test on the desk, and said good-bye to high school forever.

I didn't care about pretenses anymore—high school was history, and I felt like flaunting my freedom. That attitude came through loud and clear in the "Senior Wills" read on Class Day the final week of school. I had two bequests:

> *I, Becky Jacobs, leave my menthol cigarettes to Mr. Rioni.*
> *And . . .*
> *We, Becky Jacobs and Penny Wilson, leave the everlasting foam of our beer to the junior class, to help them through their hard-boozing years to come.*

Graduation night itself was more a downer than it was a celebration. For years, whenever I'd dreamed ahead to graduation, I imagined a night full of shared memories and nostalgia—laughing and crying with friends as we relived three, six, maybe even thirteen years of school together.

But as I marched into the gymnasium to the strains of "Pomp and Circumstance," I looked at the backs of the people marching in front of me and realized most of them were strangers. When we took our seats, I looked around. Sure, I saw a few friends, but everyone sitting there in those black robes had been a year ahead of me for the first eleven years of school. The people I shared my memories with weren't even invited to my graduation unless they came to see a brother or sister get a diploma.

A NEW START   63

When it was over there were congratulations and happy hugs from family and a few of my friends. I felt a little like an uninvited guest at a dinner party of strangers. And as if my letdown feelings weren't enough of a bummer, when I went to the office to turn in my robe and mortarboard, my guidance counselor walked up and told me that next week he would be mailing home an absence report and all the parental excuses he'd received from me during the year.

Great, I thought, *now I'll have to be home when the mail comes so I can intercept that package.* I knew my mom would be upset if she ever found out how many Mondays I'd missed—and how many times I'd forged notes with her signature.

Oh, well. What can they do to me now? I've graduated! Besides, I have a graduation party to worry about.

By all rights, graduation night should have been a party to end all parties. We had rented a big country club facility and lots of people pitched in for booze. But I felt even more out of place at the party than I had at the commencement. There was a lot of nostalgia, but it wasn't mine. So I entertained myself by getting as drunk as I could.

The only time I felt included all night, I wished I hadn't been. Someone started shoving people into the pool and I went for a sudden, unwanted swim. My glasses flew off when I hit the water, and before I could grab them they sank to the bottom of the pool.

For the next fifteen minutes I dove again and again where I thought I saw something on the bottom. Each dive into the chilly depths of the pool sobered me a little more. By the time I finally climbed out of the pool with my glasses clutched in my hand, I felt cold, weak, and depressingly sober. For me, the party was over. So I drove myself home alone at only 2:30 in the morning, asking myself the question, *Can this be all there is to it?*

I spent that summer working at Denny's during the days and partying almost every night. But I wasn't having nearly as much fun doing it as I had the year before. Probably because I no longer felt certain about the future.

I was stranded between two groups. The friends my age were all excited about starting their senior year of high school. My older friends were making all the final arrangements for college. I couldn't go back to high school, and even though I'd been accepted at nearby Northern Illinois University (NIU), I wasn't so sure I was ready for college.

One night in late July, after a few weeks of thinking about it, I made my decision. "I'm not going to NIU this fall," I announced abruptly to my mother as she stood at the kitchen sink. "I think I'd like to sit out and work for a year."

Mom and I both knew we couldn't survive in the same house together much longer—that was why we'd decided on my graduating a year early. So her answer surprised me: "I think that might be a wise decision, Becky."

Then she proposed an alternative I'd never thought of. "Why don't we call your sister in Wisconsin and see if you can live up there for the year?"

We made the call a few minutes later. My sister, Susie, liked the idea. And I began to make plans to move.

A number of my girlfriends got together and gave me a surprise going-away party—complete with cake, good-luck banners, and a memory book in which they each wrote words of tribute and encouragement. I got so loaded on beer and nostalgia that I laughed until I cried and cried until I laughed. I'd never felt so loved and affirmed in my life. To preserve the evening I made certain to have my picture taken with each of my friends; most of the snapshots caught me shamelessly mugging for the camera, an arm around a friend, a beer hoisted in one hand and a cigarette hanging from the other. There couldn't have been a better send-off.

Arriving a few days later in Madison, Wisconsin, I made the unsettling discovery that for the first time in my life, I was living in a place where I didn't know anyone my own age. Since my sister, Susie, had gone away to college the same year I'd started first grade, I didn't know her either. Even though she'd agreed to my moving to Madison, partly to help out my folks and partly to get to know me, I was determined to be independent.

For starters, I needed a job and a place of my own. The first proved quick and easy; I found a clerical job at an insurance company right next to the apartment complex where Susie lived. And since Susie managed the apartment complex, I took an apartment there as soon as I found a roommate to split the rent with me. Life once more seemed to be rolling my way.

My new roommate, Martha, was a senior at the University of Wisconsin. She introduced me to a lot of her college friends, and since I also had made friends at work, I soon had two social lives.

Hockey fans were part of Martha's college crowd, and that year the University of Wisconsin's hockey team won the national championship; so I spent a lot of time celebrating with Martha and her friends in loud, rowdy hockey bars. My own friends at work partied in a completely different style. The after-work cocktail-hour scene offered more sophisticated adventures than I'd known in high school.

Both crowds made me feel older, more mature than when I was back in Chicago. I now truly belonged in the working world, and the most wonderful thing about my independence was not having anyone to nag me about where I was going or with whom.

My roommate never became a close friend, but she was there when I just wanted someone to talk to. She was there when I really needed someone—like I did the night of my office Christmas party.

The partying began at the office early in the afternoon. I was pretty far gone by the time the office closed and everyone headed for a company-wide reception at a party room of a hotel across town. After a few more cups of Christmas punch, the milling crowd and the constant chatter seemed more than I could follow. So I wandered into a cloakroom and passed out. When I opened my eyes sometime later I decided I must be even drunker than I thought because the entire roomful of coats was a fuzzy blur. I reached to push up my glasses and rub my eyes and suddenly realized why my vision was so blurry—I had lost my glasses.

Ten minutes later one of the company executives I had spoken to only a couple of times came in to retrieve his coat and found me crawling around the cloakroom, feeling under the coatracks.

"Looking for something?" he asked.

"My glasses. I lost my glasses and I can't see to go home without them."

"Let me see if I can help find them." He got down on the floor and looked around. After a few minutes, he stood up again. "How would it be if I took you home?"

The man was as old as my father, in his fifties, professional, distinguished. "Sure," I agreed. "That would be real nice."

He helped me put on my coat and guided me to his car. I told him where I lived and we'd only begun the drive when he asked, "How would you like to stop for another drink? It'd give us a chance to talk and get to know each other."

"Okay," I said. He seemed like he was only trying to be nice, and I didn't want to be unfriendly, nor did I want to turn down a free drink.

We stopped at a bar and he led me to a corner table. But we never got to talk. I downed one drink and promptly passed out on the table. The next thing I knew, the man was half-leading, half-carrying me out to the car, saying, "I think we'd better get you home."

My roommate opened our apartment door, looking at surprise at my escort. "She had a little too much to drink at our company party," he explained quickly. "She lost her glasses somewhere at the hotel, and I wanted to make sure she made it home okay."

As soon as he left, Martha stripped my clothes off me and put me in a tub of cool water until my head began to clear. When I was sober enough to tell her what hotel we had been at for the party, she insisted on driving me there to look again for my glasses. We soon found them in one of the back corners of the cloakroom and I returned home feeling terribly hung over and grateful for my roommate's help.

The one area of my life I wasn't satisfied with was my love life. Or rather my lack of it. One morning shortly after Christmas, as I dressed for work and stepped in front of a mirror for a final check, the problem hit me. The reason I didn't have a boyfriend was obvious. With all the drinking I was doing, plus the fact I was eating a lot more snacks than healthy meals living on my own, I had ballooned to 150 pounds. I looked fat—and I felt fatter.

Embarrassed at the thought of ever going back home looking as I did, I went on a crash diet. No fatty foods, no snacks, and no booze. I went cold turkey. After twenty-five days, I had lost 25 pounds and gained a heavy supply of attention and affirmation.

Feeling good about my weight again, I had no reason not to drink. Mixed drinks were my new favorites—strong and fast acting. Sometimes they hit me too hard; at least once a weekend I would pass out and one of my friends would have to drive me home.

After six months or so the price of my independence seemed awfully high. The bills kept piling up, and the cost of living climbed faster than my total take-home pay. College life looked more and more appealing. And I came to the conclusion I needed more education to be a true success in life.

One dark February day I called home. When Mom answered I said, "Hi, Mom. It's Becky. I want to come home."

"To do what?" I could tell she wasn't happy about the prospect.

"I'd like to start spring quarter at NIU next month."

"That'll cost money, Becky. I don't think we have enough money to pay your tuition right now." I could tell she wanted to talk me out of it.

"I can pay my tuition," I said. "I've got a little money saved, and I'll have a couple more paychecks before I come home."

"Okay," Mom agreed reluctantly. "If you can pay your tuition, I guess you can come home."

So I gave notice at my job, told Martha she'd have to find another roommate, and began making plans to head home. But my new plans for the future didn't keep me from remembering the excitement I'd felt only months before when my Chicago friends had sent me packing on my Wisconsin adventure. I tried to act excited about starting college. Doing so made it easier to explain my decision to my friends and helped ease the sense of failure I felt at so soon giving up on my new working lifestyle.

CHAPTER 7

LOSING GROUND

After I'd spent a few days at home, my folks loaded my stuff in the car and drove me the hour to Northern Illinois University, where I was to attend my first quarter. I was finally a college girl.

It seemed as if half my high school was at NIU. So it was easy to find people to party with every weekend.

But I studied, too. Every night—from Monday through Thursday—I holed up in the library. I was determined to prove myself, to show my parents I could succeed if I set my mind to it. When grades came out at the end of the quarter I had a perfect 4.0 average.

As further evidence of my responsibility, when I came home for the summer I landed a full-time summer job in the downtown Chicago office of an insurance firm—a branch of the company I'd worked for in Wisconsin. And the pay was even better than before. I wrote in my journal:

> I'm excited to begin a new job, but even more elated to go to work from nine to five. At five o'clock my worries, problems, and responsibilities end! What I'm really trying to say is that I'll have no homework, or tests, or assignments to begin or finish after working hours.

If my parents were reassured by my good grades and my ability to find steady work, I very quickly let them know my newfound successes didn't mean I still couldn't do what I wanted. After almost a year away from my hometown, I had a lot of catching up to do. The entire summer served as one long reunion/celebration party. I awakened most mornings nursing a hangover, and my mother's periodic nagging produced the same effect as trying to douse a campfire with gasoline. I don't think either of us thought we would survive the summer in the same house.

Fall finally came, and I returned to school to discover that my academic showing the previous spring had earned me the honor of membership in the university's honor sorority, Alpha Lambda Delta. My parents accepted the school's invitation to attend the induction ceremony and a special reception with the school's administration.

I think the occasion offered my parents a glimmer of hope, a surprising moment of parental pride after almost three years of frustration and disappointment. As the speaker droned on about values like leadership and commitment, I looked around at the girls being inducted with me and felt terribly uncomfortable and out of place—partly because I realized I was wearing a dress for the first time since I'd come to college, but mostly because none of these honor roll students were my friends, nor did I want them to be. So when my name was called and I had to walk across the stage to receive a rose and a certificate of membership, it seemed more of an embarrassment than an honor.

After that ceremony, my motivation for studying began to erode. Consequently, I spent a lot more of my fall term partying than I spent in the library.

Ben and Alex, the two Arlington guys Trish had introduced me to, were both NIU students that fall. So when they took up rugby playing, my suitemate Connie and I got interested in the rugby scene.

A lot of ex-high-school football players, those who weren't quite dedicated enough for college football, joined the university rugby club. There would be a match almost every Saturday against the rugby team of some other midwestern university. It always took place on some peripheral college field, where the periodic, distant roar of the crowd crammed into the football stadium could be heard. Rugby, though fiercely competitive, was much more a fraternal, social happening than it was a public spectacle.

On Saturday night, after the match, both teams and their friends would get together and party. And on Sunday, before the visiting team members headed home to their campus, the home team would host a big picnic for the visitors. There would be kegs of beer to drink and everyone would get blasted.

Perhaps the biggest event of the fall came when Connie and I traveled down to Champaign to stay with one of Connie's friends for the University of Illinois's homecoming celebration. We arrived at the U of I campus midafternoon on Friday in order to get the earliest possible start on two straight days of partying.

Late Friday afternoon we sat in a dorm room, waiting for Connie's friend Dawn to finish dressing for our night on the town. Dawn paused in the middle of applying her mascara and reached into a dresser drawer. Pulling out a small vial of pills, she asked, "You ever try Quaalude, Becky?"

"No," I responded. "What'll it do?"

"Everything slows down," she said. "Like slow motion. And then you'll laugh and laugh. Try one."

So I took it and waited for something to happen. "How long does it take?" I asked after a few minutes.

"Depends," Dawn answered. "Usually not long. Aren't you feeling anything?"

"I don't think so."

We left for town a few minutes later. By the time we reached the first bar, I decided the Quaalude wasn't going to affect me and began downing beer until I was rip-roaring drunk. Then the Quaalude finally hit and hit hard. I don't remember going back to the dorm.

I woke up very late the next morning, with such a bad hangover I had to drink a few beers to numb the pain enough to make the football game. I drank some more while I watched, and that evening went out for some serious partying. Dawn and Connie met and hit it off with a couple of guys. When they left together, I went with some students I'd met during the evening back to their dorm, where we finished off a variety of hard liquor they had stashed in their room. It was a mixed group and one of the guys made a few passes at me. He was cute, so we necked for a while until I passed out.

When I opened my eyes, the strange surroundings came slowly into focus and I remembered the party. Trying to judge the time by the semidarkness outside the window I thought, *It can't be too long until dawn. Dawn. Where is she? I don't even know where her dorm is from here.* Quickly and quietly, I got to my feet and tried to stand perfectly still until the room stopped spinning. Then I slipped out of the room, down the hall, and out into the chill of a fall morning. For the next half hour I wandered around the campus without another soul in sight, searching for a building that looked like Dawn's dorm.

When I finally found it and let myself in, Connie and Dawn were still asleep. I lay down and promptly went to sleep myself, waking up just in time to catch our mid-day ride back to NIU.

"We had a great weekend," Connie and I assured Dawn as we bid her good-bye. But as the Illinois farm country rolled by outside the car window on the way back, I had to acknowledge a real sense of disappointment. I couldn't remember enough of the weekend to recall what had been so great about it.

I spent a lot of my time at NIU with my suitemate Connie. She'd go to a lot of the rugby parties with me, and we'd go out together many weekends. But as the quarter wore on, I began to wonder whether we wouldn't be better friends if we didn't live so close to each other.

Connie was the kind of girl who had everything going for her. She climbed out of bed in the morning with every hair in place. Her parents were rich and she had so many clothes she could go for weeks without repeating an outfit. She'd offer to let me borrow anything I liked in her closet, but we both knew it would never fit. She'd been blessed with one of those petite and shapely figures that never seemed to change no matter how many candy bars or ice cream sundaes she consumed.

Guys she met in class would call her up for dates, but she turned most of them down. She not only had self-confidence, but to top it all off, she had the self-discipline and brains to make good grades, too.

She never flaunted what she had. But I knew she knew she had it all. And as the quarter passed, that grated on me.

The one area in which I could outdo her was drinking. I kept the refrigerator in our suite stashed full of little seven-ounce beer bottles we called "Little Mickeys." We'd often get a group together on our floor to play the drinking board game "Pass Out" before we went out partying at the local bars. But Connie always seemed to be holding back in our drinking contests, never willing to let go and lose control. I'd begin my weekend partying on Thursday nights, but Connie would wait until Friday. So she didn't miss many Friday classes like I did.

I built quite a reputation as a drinker—putting away as many as twelve to fifteen beers a night, four nights a week. Drinking was the social ticket that not only helped me fit in, it got me in. On Sunday afternoons, for example, Doug and John, a couple of friends from home—the same two guys Wendy and I had run around with the summer before my sophomore year—would invite me to their fraternity house. There five or six of us would watch the football games on television and drain a whole keg of beer bought for the occasion. I'd usually be the only girl there, but they'd treat me like one of the guys because they knew I could drink with the best of them.

I remember running into Doug at a bar in town and having him introduce me to his friends. "She'll fit right in," he assured them. "She's a real lush."

Everyone laughed. And I laughed along with them. I was so glad to have Doug's friendship and acceptance that I didn't think of it as a derogatory comment. I still had something of a crush on Doug since that Fourth of July night years before when he'd given me my first grown-up kiss. I kept looking for some clue that he felt the same thing toward me. From time to time I thought I noticed more than a fraternal, drinking-buddy feeling in his attitude toward me. But when I'd respond by clinging to him at parties, or asking him to slow dance, he'd back off and act cool toward me for the next few days.

My academic life went the way of my social life. My grades dropped to 3.0 for the fall and kept right on going down as winter quarter started. A couple of weeks into January I dropped my anatomy class because I could tell it was going to require too much studying just to pass. That left me with only three classes, the minimum load I could carry and still be considered a full-time student with the privilege of living in the dorm.

Connie and I remained friends, but we spent less and less time together. She studied even more than she had in the fall—and I hardly studied at all. We'd go out on some weekends, but she almost always left the bar or the party before I really got started. She stuck to her personal rules of only drinking on weekends despite the fact that I would start partying on Wednesday nights now, instead of Thursday nights.

One blustery, cold Monday evening in January when I was feeling bored, I remembered Monday was ladies' night in the downtown bars. I didn't even bother asking Connie; instead I went up and down the hall asking if anyone would like to go to town with me for a few drinks. Everyone was busy.

I walked back to my room disappointed, thinking, *I'm not going out drinking alone!* But I felt the need for a drink and I no sooner flopped down on my bed and picked up a textbook than I decided to go anyway. *I'll find someone I know in town,* I assured myself as I bundled up and hurried out of the dorm.

I stopped right inside the bar door and waited for my eyes to adjust to the light. Then as nonchalantly as I could, I slipped to the bar, climbed up on a stool, and coolly ordered a beer. I turned and surveyed the entire establishment as if I were looking or waiting for someone who was supposed to meet me there. After three or four beers, two college kids walked in—not actually friends, but people I knew by name.

I waved, and seeing I wasn't with anyone else, they motioned me over. I drank a few more beers and made small talk with them for a while before heading back to campus by myself, satisfied that at least I hadn't had to drink alone. It paid to have friends!

But I wasn't fooling myself. I admitted my growing discouragement in a daily journal my English instructor assigned us to keep.

Sunday seems the traditional day of the week for rest and depression.

Today was really slow and sad. I felt like I just wanted to go home and stay there for an endless period of time. I longed for my own soft bed and a long, hot bath. I am homesick.

Even watching *The Wizard of Oz* made me feel worse. Like knowing I've grown up too quickly and will never be ten years old again.

The next day I wrote:

Today resembled a fuzzy daydream. I kept napping, then awakening in a dazed world. I felt physically and mentally ill, and kept wondering if the previous day's depression had this effect. I felt useless, like I had no real purpose or function in living.

And a few days later:

I leave myself with this one thought to look back on: This week has been so depressing, it couldn't get any worse!

Depression seemed to be taking its toll in various ways. And my journal recorded my deepening malaise:

I fail to understand why I sleep in the afternoon when I should be studying and then try to study late at night when I should be sleeping. (Any explanations?)

Determination involves self-discipline. How can a person improve on his self-discipline?

One Saturday morning I caught a ride home with Doug and John and a couple of their friends. The plan was just to do laundry, go to the bank, run a few errands, and say hi to a few friends before heading back to school in time to party that night. However, on the drive back to school in the late afternoon, we got an early start on the partying when we stopped and picked up a case of beer to drink on the way.

About halfway back to NIU, I got desperate for a bathroom stop. Doug laughed, and making some comment about not being able to hold my beer, threatened to see if I could make it all the way back to campus. When I convinced him I was desperate, he pulled off at the next exit and wheeled into a Holiday Inn parking lot.

As I closed the door and hurried into the lobby, I heard one of the guys in the backseat say, "Why don't we just leave her here?" I felt sure he was just kidding, but not absolutely certain.

When I hurried out a few minutes later and found the car gone, I felt a surge of panic. I strained, looking up and down the parking lot. Nothing. I figured it was just a joke, but I still felt hurt and insecure. When I finally spotted them parked around the corner of the building, they all laughed. I didn't think it was funny and began to worry that maybe they *didn't* like me.

My relationship with Connie seemed to be deteriorating as well. We never had any real fights—just a lot of silence—and we spent less and less time together.

I would try to get her to go with me to parties. "Doug would sure like to see you," I'd tell her. Doug did have something of a crush on her. I was beginning to think maybe that was his only interest in me—just a way to get next to Connie. I decided if that was true, I couldn't blame him for using me. I was using Connie, too. The main reason I wanted her to go with me to parties wasn't that I wanted her company, but because I knew she was someone people wanted at a party. She was my ticket. If people liked me it was because they liked her.

Without her I felt out of place and unwanted at parties, and I ended up drinking more than ever to wipe out those feelings of insecurity.

I did get invited to a big frat party one Saturday near the end of the term. The guests, including a number of visitors I didn't know from U of I, made the beer disappear almost as fast as the hosts could roll out a new keg. And as usual, I downed more than my share.

The fraternity guys began singing drinking songs with the crudest lyrics I'd ever heard in my life. The drinking and the singing looked as if they'd go on all night. I had more beers than I could count and began to feel very woozy. So, leaving the booze and bawdiness behind, I wandered into a bedroom, climbed onto a mountain of coats on the bed, and promptly dozed off.

I came to as someone roughly rolled me over. I opened my eyes to see a drunken guy standing over me. Another stranger's face, leering from beside him, came slowly into focus as I felt their hands and realized what was going on. They were pulling off my clothes!

Suddenly sober and wide awake, I kicked at them and screamed.

"Get away! Leave me alone!"

Now they were laughing. One of them pinned me down. My screams weren't much of a defense.

The next instant, a familiar face appeared at the doorway. "What's—"

"Doug! Help me! Please! Help!" I screamed.

As Doug stepped into the room, the two guys backed away. I jumped to my feet, pulled my clothes back into place, grabbed my coat, and bolted out of the party.

Shocked and badly shaken by what had almost happened,

I ran back to my room. There I wept in despair at the realization of how messed up my life was. My grades were plummeting. I didn't have any friends. Now this.

I felt more down, more defeated than ever before. Knowing there was no way I could go on, I got up the next morning and called home.

"I'm quitting school," I told my mom. "I want to come home." I couldn't bring myself to add "again."

There was a long silence on the other end of the line before my mother asked, "How are we going to make it?"

"I'll be busy," I assured her. "I'll work downtown and take classes part-time at the University of Illinois Circle Campus. I'll have to study. I won't be around much. It won't be like before."

My mother sighed. "I don't know . . ."

"I'll change," I promised. "You'll see. I'll obey you. I'll do whatever you want me to do. I'll get it together there. I just want to come home."

Another long silence. "Okay."

So I packed up my things, bummed a ride back home with a friend, and never went back to Northern Illinois University again. I never even told Connie or my other suitemates that I was leaving.

CHAPTER 8

CALIFORNIA CROSSROADS

I don't even remember when I started to dream about California. I think it was sometime about the middle of the summer. During spring quarter at Circle I'd held down a part-time job at the same insurance office where I'd worked the summer before. Once school got out, I took a full-time position for the summer. But it wasn't long before I felt ready for a drastic change of scenery.

I spent much of my time that summer with Sarah, a new friend from work. We'd often go out for dinner and then go out drinking and dancing at our favorite downtown haunt, a nightclub called Faces. I slept at Sarah's a lot of nights to avoid going home and facing my parents; that relationship seemed to be worsening again.

It was at Faces one evening that I began talking to Sarah about my daydreams of traveling west. And the more I talked, the better and more realistic it all sounded.

Freedom. Sunshine. Beach boys. Fun. Freedom. My friends encouraged me—but my family didn't. I don't think anyone really took me seriously. Yet the talk continued, and California seemed closer and closer. California. That's where I needed to go to start over, to show everyone—my parents, my friends, myself—that Becky Jacobs was in control of her life. That Becky Jacobs could make it—could be someone in this world.

I borrowed money from my brother, Fred, to buy an old VW Rabbit. Then I took out a loan for five hundred dollars so I'd have some start-up money in California.

Sarah was leaving the insurance company to go back to school. She had three free weeks before her fall term started, so she decided to drive to California with me to see the country.

So on Labor Day, the two of us packed my car to the ceiling with my earthly possessions, said good-bye to our families, and headed for the westbound interstate.

We zigzagged our way cross-country—from Illinois to Wisconsin to Missouri to Colorado—staying with friends and relatives to save money. And as we traveled on our quest for sun, surfers, and happiness, the radio often blared out a rock tune I took as an omen and adopted as my personal theme song:

We've been waiting for the sun to rise and shine
Shining still to give us the will
Somehow, someday, we need just one victory
  and we're on our way
Prayin' for it all day and fightin' for it all night
Give us just one victory and it will be all right.

I knew when I got to California I would turn my life around. I needed "just one victory," one success, and I could prove myself once and for all. I would find that in California and I wouldn't go back to Illinois until I could return with my head held high. In fact, I made myself a vow that I would never again call home in defeat like I had after Wisconsin and college.

Our last stop before the coast was Las Vegas, where we splurged on a room at the Desert Inn. We didn't have enough money to see any of the shows, but we decided to risk a few bucks just so we could say we gambled in Vegas.

A stranger in the casino gave me a chip; I put it down on the crap table and promptly won twenty dollars. For me, that was another good omen; even luck was going my way. With my winnings I treated Sarah to a big buffet breakfast the next morning before we left on the last leg of our trip to the coast.

The first thing we did when we reached southern California that afternoon was to stop at the beach, since Sarah had never seen the Pacific. I called a cousin of mine who lived in LA and she called her friends and organized an impromptu beach party for us.

That night as the sun set in the Pacific, Sarah and I took off our shoes, waded out into the surf, and celebrated our successful transcontinental journey by singing "Just One Victory" to the stars. Then we lit a bonfire, roasted hot dogs, and I loaded up on booze until I began to feel sick.

"I gotta lie down," I told Sarah, wishing I didn't have to miss out on the fun.

She and my cousin half-carried me over to the parking lot and helped me into the back of my cousin's pickup. I once awakened just enough to lean over the side and throw up and to see silhouettes milling around the fire on the beach. But it wasn't until I roused the next morning at my cousin's house that I felt regrets. To think I'd spent my first glorious night in California in the back of a pickup, sleeping off a drunken binge. Why did I always overdo it?

After a week of sightseeing in southern California, Sarah flew home to begin school and I headed up the coast to my ultimate destination—central California. I had an uncle and aunt who were retired and lived in Pebble Beach.

Uncle Tim had been a career military man—a lieutenant colonel when he retired. Aunt Martha was a blonde, sophisticated woman who had lived on military bases around the world.

They hadn't seen me for more than four years—back when I'd been the all-American cheerleader. They weren't prepared for the new me. I climbed out of the car to greet them wearing the same brown flannel shirt, blue-jean cutoffs, and flip-flops I'd worn most of the three-thousand-mile trip. My hair was dirty, and I had gained thirteen pounds on our thirteen-day trip from washing down fast-food hamburgers with whatever cheap brew I could drink on the way.

I sensed the last thing Aunt Martha wanted to do was hug me, but she did. And she welcomed me into her home. She and Uncle Tim even offered me a place to stay until I found work and a place to live.

Good jobs proved a lot harder to come by than I'd counted on. However, within a few days I landed a job doing data entry for a small company in Seaside. The pay wasn't as much as I'd hoped for but enough to afford a small furnished apartment. Once I had work and a place to live I finally was ready to begin a serious search for my California dream: sunshine, beach boys, fun, freedom.

California is a twenty-one state, so as a nineteen-year-old I wasn't old enough to drink. However, I heard about a military bar at a nearby military installation that would admit eighteen year olds. Friends at work said most of the clientele came from the DLI—the Defense Language Institute—where the American Armed Forces train translators—all about my age!

Booze and boys. It sounded to me like the perfect combination, and I checked the place out the very next weekend. I found plenty of beer, dancing, and a highly favorable ratio of guys to girls. I quickly hit it off with two young soldiers studying at the DLI and was only mildly disappointed to discover they weren't big surfers. In fact, the first guys I met after I'd driven clear across the country dreaming of blond, surfing hunks, were from Gary, Indiana!

My Las Vegas luck was still holding out because that very night those same guys introduced me to Tina, a girl who just happened to be looking for someone with an apartment to share. Ironically, she too was from Illinois (Peoria) and had been in California working as a waitress for about three months. She moved in with me two days later, and suddenly with someone to share the expenses, my California dream came back into focus.

The next week we invited the DLI guys to our place for a big party. And in the weeks that followed we made our apartment their home away from home—a place they were welcome to crash when they got off duty and wanted to escape the military regimen.

Through those guys and people we met at work, we soon

had a big circle of friends. Within weeks our apartment was Party Central. Any night we decided to have a party, people just showed up. Often they stayed and slept on the living room floor.

One night, a couple of guys who had motorcycles stayed over. The next morning Todd, a friend of mine, suggested that the two of us go for a ride. So I got high smoking dope and we left the apartment together. A few minutes later, cruising down the highway with the wind whipping through my hair, I realized I was still wearing my flannel pajamas. I threw back my head and laughed in exhilaration. For the first time in my life I could do whatever I wanted to do, when I wanted to do it, without being hassled by anyone. I was having so much fun in the present that I seldom thought about the past or the people I'd left behind—until one fall Saturday evening.

I had some friends over and was just getting down to some serious drinking when I heard a loud commotion from outside our apartment. I stepped out on our patio and heard it again—the sound of a cheering crowd. Climbing to the top of our six-foot-high, brick privacy wall, I spotted the source of the noise.

"Hey, look at this," I called to the others. There, directly below our high, hillside apartment, was the Central California Junior College football field—and a game was just getting under way.

"We got great seats," I said. "Can somebody hand me up a beer? Or maybe a six-pack."

For the next two-and-a-half hours we perched atop our wall, drinking our beer, and cheering our heads off for the home team. None of us knew a soul down there on that field. The game was nothing more than an evening's diversion. Yet, as I watched the players collide on the field, their school colors intensified by the bright lights, and faintly heard the cheerleaders working the crowd, old memories and emotions surged up from my subconscious, where I'd kept them buried for so long. For a few moments, sitting on that wall, I was actually more than two thousand miles away. And when

I "returned to California" I couldn't help but wonder, *What if . . . ?*

When the final gun sounded and we all scrambled down off the wall to our patio, someone said, "We'll have to do this again."

"Sure," I said, but I didn't mean it. And we never did. As Christmas approached I think Tina and I thought a lot about home. We decided not to let a lack of money dampen our Christmas spirit. Since the cost of buying a tree was prohibitive, I borrowed a hatchet. Late one night I drove with a DLI friend from work up the mountain behind the college where, under cover of darkness, we felled a small pine tree. Watching for headlights, we hurriedly stashed our tree in the back of my Rabbit and drove right home. Back in the safety of our parking lot, we laughed hilariously at our adventure for several minutes before we regained strength enough to haul my prize into the apartment.

At a craft store I purchased a pattern for making wooden ornaments to decorate our tree. Tina bought felt and we made each other stockings with our names on them. Then we filled the stockings with inexpensive items such as barrettes and socks. In defense against loneliness, we became our own little family and tried to re-create a traditional Christmas for ourselves.

On Christmas Eve we held our family celebration and invited a couple of military guys who hadn't been able to get leaves to go home. The four of us ate together and the guys stayed and sat with us by the tree as Tina and I opened our presents. Tina had received a big package from home with a number of presents. I received one present from my folks—a robe. We took turns opening and exclaiming over our gifts, periodically stopping to toast one another with a glass of wine.

I felt pretty sentimental (not to mention drunk) when Aunt Martha called and invited us to join her and Uncle Tim at their church's midnight Christmas Eve service. "Sure," I told her. Going to church would only make it seem more like Christmas.

The guys headed back to the base, and one of my cousins came by to pick up Tina and me. I saw him eyeing us uncomfortably as we giggled all the way to the church. I sobered up enough to follow the usher down the center aisle. I was about to decide he was going to seat us in the choir loft when he finally stopped just a few pews from the front and motioned us to sit beside Aunt Martha.

I remember standing to sing "Silent Night," and I recall a choir in red robes. But that's it. The service had hardly begun before I went sound asleep on Tina's shoulder. She told me later it was all she could do to keep from cracking up right there in the service.

I hate to think what Aunt Martha thought about it, but I didn't ask, and she didn't mention it the next day when she had us over for Christmas dinner.

The only thing that ever cramped our partying style was money—or lack of it. Despite Tina's contribution to expenses and a surprising raise at the office, I never seemed to have any extra money. Partying is expensive, especially if it's your party. By the time I'd stockpiled our booze, there wasn't enough cash left over to cover rent, utilities, gasoline, medical bills, and groceries. So we often skimped on groceries.

One night in January the only food we had in the house was a can of mushrooms. We sautéed them in our last half stick of butter and ate them for supper—along with an entire bottle of good California wine. When we finished eating, Tina hurried off to the restaurant to fill in on a late shift for a friend. I collapsed on the couch to watch TV.

I was still there when the buzzer sounded. I opened the door to find my brother, Fred, standing there. He had come to pay me a surprise visit.

As a golf pro back home, he'd accepted an offer from Uncle Tim to take an extended winter golf vacation in Pebble Beach. I saw Fred eyeing the leftover mushrooms and the wine on our supper table. His veiled surprise changed to obvious awkwardness when I lit up a joint.

"Want some?" I asked as I passed him the cigarette. "It's good stuff."

"No, thanks," he replied quickly, obviously wanting nothing to do with my pot. His face conveyed his next thought, even before he voiced the words. "You've changed, Becky."

"I've grown up, Fred." He'd been away in the service the entire time I'd been in high school. To him, I was still his kid sister, the little junior high girl in braces.

I told him all about my job and about the friends I'd made since I got to California. I wanted to reassure him that I was a big girl now—someone who could take care of herself. We agreed to stay in touch and do some fun things together while he was in California.

Before he left that night to go back to my aunt and uncle's he gave me a big hug and warned in a brotherly, teasing voice, "You better be careful, Becky." I was about to reassure him one last time when he added, "You're getting a little fat, aren't you?"

Those words, coming from the big brother I'd idolized all my life, the handsome quarterback with the cheerleading girlfriend, cut me to the bone. I started a diet the very next day, but I didn't try to change the lifestyle I knew he disapproved of.

My lifestyle left me so strapped that I had no choice but to write home and ask my parents for loans to get me through the end of the month. It was about that time my big, bright California dream began to fade. I didn't particularly like my work. I had a growing dissatisfaction with my job not only because I did not get paid enough, but because I also had to put up with a few married men who hassled me at the office. That, plus the financial hole I'd gotten into, started me thinking. *This is not what I had in mind when I came to California! Something has got to change—and fast.*

Tina had come to California with her own dreams, but she was ready to trade them in for something bigger.

"Alaska!" she said one night. "Let's go to Alaska, Becky. The worst job up there pays better than we're making now.

When summer comes we could get a three-month job on the pipeline and make a fortune!"

Normally I'd have gone along with anything—in fact, I was usually the instigator of such ideas. But not this time. In fact, the more Tina talked about Alaska during the next few days, the more uneasy I felt. I knew jobs were scarce in Alaska, and even though the high pay was enticing, I also knew that the living expenses were just as high—or higher. There was no way I was going to let myself get stranded in the Arctic circle with no alternative but to call my family and ask them to fly me home. I knew my parents couldn't afford that, and neither could I. Besides, I'd promised myself that I would never again call and ask Mom and Dad if I could come back home.

So I just listened for a few days as Tina's talk quickly changed from verbal daydreaming to serious planning. I didn't tell her I wouldn't go. I didn't want to lose her friendship. Not to mention that, without a roommate, I'd be hard-pressed to make ends meet financially. *Maybe something will happen,* I thought. *Maybe she'll change her mind, or something else will come along.* But as the days went on, I started to feel as if my California dream was collapsing around me.

CHAPTER 9

PURSUING THE VICTORY

I finally got fed up with my job and quit early in February after receiving my income tax refund check. Tina figured that meant I would go along with her Alaska plans and promptly made plane reservations for both of us for the first of March. She gave notice at work she'd be leaving, but I decided to look around for a different job.

There weren't many. Most of them were dead-end jobs no better than I'd had before. The one possible exception was a job I heard about from a friend—a position in the office of a local Buick dealership. I applied and set up an interview with the business manager, a Mrs. Felton, for that Friday.

When I awakened on Thursday, I felt as if the weight of uncertainty would smother me. There seemed to be a growing fear deep inside me. I had only one prospect left, and that was a long shot. I couldn't stay in California by myself. Nor could I go to Alaska with Tina. I was stuck with choosing the lesser of two evils.

No nearer a good solution after an eternity under the covers, I finally forced myself to get up. Pulling on my Central High cheerleader jacket, my most faded blue jeans, and a pair of sandals, I walked out of the apartment, climbed into my car, and began to drive. I had no idea where I was going. I just had to think.

My car and my mind wandered for over an hour, until I was ready to give up and go back to the apartment. And that's just about the time I noticed a roadside sign indicating a church ahead—of the denomination in which I grew up. I hadn't been to church in ages except for Christmas Eve, when I'd been so drunk I'd slept through the service.

There's no one else to talk to, I thought. *I can't go to Uncle Tim and Aunt Martha; they'll just talk about responsibility, perseverance, and things like that. They won't understand the total picture, my loyalty to Tina or to my dream.* While I debated with myself, I followed the arrow on the sign and pulled to a stop in the empty parking lot.

I sat in my car for a few minutes, reluctant to follow my crazy impulse. But something seemed to be drawing me into the building. I finally opened the car door, walked into the church office, and asked the secretary, "Is the pastor in today?"

A few minutes later I sat in a book-lined office, looking across a cluttered desk at a kind-looking, gray-haired stranger and wondering what in the world to say.

"My name is Becky Jacobs," I began. "I'm from Chicago, Illinois, but I've been living out here for about six months now. I haven't been to church very much in recent years, and I'm going through a very confusing time in my life."

The man nodded slightly. "What is it that's troubling you?"

I explained my basic problem—that Tina was going to Alaska and I hadn't been able to tell her I couldn't go. I explained that I'd quit my job and that California now looked as bleak as the North Pole. I told him about the interview scheduled for the next day and about the plane reservations we had in two weeks.

I poured out my confusion there in that quiet office, and I almost begged him to make some decisions for me.

When I finished, the minister sat for a few moments in silence. Then he kindly looked into my eyes and said, "Becky, if you go to that interview tomorrow, I believe God will speak through that woman."

The man's words stunned me. *He's joking, right? What does he mean? How could God speak to me through a woman I'd never met before?* My mind pictured a woman at a desk, her lips barely moving, with a deep megaphone voice booming out, "Becky Jacobs, don't go." I nearly grinned at the absurd image.

But as I said good-bye to the minister and thanked him for his time, my curiosity was beginning to work. I knew no matter what I was going to that interview.

"We'd be glad to have you come and worship with us on Sunday," the minister said as he walked me to the door.

"I'll think about it," I told him. But I knew I wouldn't.

That same night, only a few days after I'd quit my job, one of the girls I'd worked with called and asked me to stop by for a good-bye party. Pam was my age and a real wild character. Her idea of a friendly going-away gesture was to have a few hits of LSD.

I had always steered clear of hard drugs. But she said it would be a great high, so I took what looked like a small piece of granular sugar candy, which Pam peeled off a strip of wax paper. Then we sat around her apartment waiting for the LSD to begin to work.

The hallucinations came so quickly they scared me. When I looked at my hands, I didn't see any fingers. I tried to pick up the phone to call for help, but the receiver kept falling out of my hand as if there really were no fingers. *It's just a bad trip*, I told myself. But the terror didn't go away. *Why can't I see my fingers?*

Everyone else at her party must have had just as wild a trip as I did, because when the drug eventually wore off, the apartment was a mess. Someone had been violent enough to break up two of the chairs. I was glad my roommate hadn't seen me like that.

I vowed never to take another hit of LSD as long as I lived. The lack of control scared me more than anything I'd ever experienced before.

I can't go on living like this, I told myself when I woke up the next morning in Pam's apartment. And that realization was one more reason to go to my interview.

Five minutes in Mrs. Felton's office at Pride Buick wiped away weeks of indecision: I wanted the job. As Mrs. Felton looked over my resumé, I felt glad I'd decided to wear the conservative navy-colored suit my mother had sent me. I'd never had it on before—too stuffy-looking for my taste, but obviously not for Mrs. Felton.

She had a firm handshake. Perfect nails. Not a hair out of place. Everything about her, from her ramrod-straight posture to her expensively tailored suit, proclaimed her personality, even before you heard her precise, clipped speech. *Here, I thought, is the most sophisticated, professional woman I've ever met.* And despite her obvious, no-nonsense personality, I instantly concluded I wanted to work for this lady.

When she finished reviewing my application, she commented on my surprising amount of experience for someone so young. Then she asked some questions about the details of my former jobs. I tried to answer in as mature and professional a voice as I could.

But I nearly lost my cool and screamed in surprised delight when she concluded the interview by saying, "I'd like to offer you the job, Rebecca."

Everything began spinning in my mind at once. "Could you wait and let me start in two weeks?" I asked, explaining that I felt responsible for getting my roommate moved out of our apartment and to the airport since I owned the only car.

"Two weeks will be just fine."

My decision was made. All that remained was to break the news to Tina.

I didn't have any time to ease into the subject. The minute she got home after work that evening, Tina asked, "What happened at your interview today?"

I took a deep breath and answered. "I took the job. I start the second of March."

She didn't say a word, but I saw the "I-knew-it" look on her face and felt her silent anger.

"I'm sorry," I said, "but try to understand. I can't go to Alaska. I couldn't ask my parents to fly me home. I just can't go. And this job is too good to pass up."

"Sure, being a company switchboard operator is a great career!" Tina quipped sarcastically.

"Mrs. Felton told me the switchboard thing could be very

temporary. The company is getting a whole new computer system when they move to their new location in four months. There's a chance that I'll be moved up then."

"You gotta do what you gotta do," Tina said. But the tone of her voice didn't convince me that she meant it. I could feel a wedge growing between us.

We never had an out-and-out fight about my decision. We didn't have to. Tina and I had always been able to tell what the other one was thinking. From the very start, that night we met in the military bar, there had been a closeness, an instant bond, between us. And that closeness had grown stronger and stronger—until Alaska cropped up. Now I could feel the coldness widening between us.

I didn't even sense any appreciation for the fact that I'd arranged my schedule so I could help her move out and drive her to the airport. When departure day finally came, we shared a few nostalgic tears at the boarding gate, but the feelings had changed. The good-byes and good lucks could not cover the rift between us.

Driving back from the airport I realized that, in spite of the hurt I felt at Tina's anger and alienation, I couldn't help envying her big Alaska adventure. *Maybe I should have gone.* No, I was excited, too, because I was embarking on a new adventure all my own. I just knew I was going to find victory in my new job at Pride Buick.

I determined to change my image completely as I started my new job. I would wear a dress or skirt almost every day, and nylons, even though I hated them.

Aunt Martha and Uncle Tim acted very pleased at my decision to stay in California. I gave up my apartment and accepted their gracious offer of a place to stay until I found another roommate, but I began to wonder if Aunt Martha wasn't out to change my image! She expected me home in time for dinner every night after work, and curfew was eleven o'clock.

The rules would have grated on me if I hadn't been so excited about my job. Within the first few weeks Mrs. Felton began to increase my responsibilities and compliment me on my hard work. Only a month or so after I started, she cosigned papers so I could purchase a brand-new car from the dealership. She obviously liked and trusted me, and I vowed to keep that trust.

Not that I gave up my good times. I just exchanged my pattern of daily binges and all-night bashes for the after-work cocktail hour at nearby bars. (By this time I had doctored my birth date on my California driver's license so I could pass for twenty-one instead of twenty).

I spent much of my drinking and party time with new friends from the dealership who were single and about my age. They talked a lot about love and sex, and what they said intrigued and confused me. I had always thought of love and sex as one and the same thing. Not so, according to my friends. And they seemed to know a lot more than I did on the subjects.

While I had kissed a lot of boys, and a number of them had probably gotten me drunk with the sole intention of lowering my defenses, the truth was that I had never gone all the way with a guy. As old-fashioned as it sounded, I somehow had managed to maintain my dream of saving myself for the one man who would be my forever true love. But as I listened to my experienced California friends talk about their sexual exploits, I began to think maybe I was foolishly naive. They really convinced me that *everyone* did it.

My new job not only gave a boost to my professional status and social life, but it also produced a blond California surfer—John, a mechanic working right at the Buick dealership. For a week or so he stopped to say hi whenever he walked by my desk. Then one day he asked me out. We had a good time, and he asked me out again. Within a few short weeks we became a regular twosome.

Every evening we went to a bar or his place until it was time to get back to Aunt Martha's. We'd take coffee breaks together, and he even arranged his lunch hour to coincide with mine. We'd go to a nearby pizza place and split a pitcher of beer with our lunch. Since he had great connections for quality marijuana, we'd often share a joint in his car before we headed back to the office.

I figured as long as I was careful and Mrs. Felton didn't find out, my lunchtime highs wouldn't hurt anything. While I continued to be concerned about my image, John was worth the risk. He was a little on the shy side and so cute—everything I'd wanted in a guy. I could hardly believe my luck, but I couldn't shake the nagging fear that he might drop me in a minute if someone else came along.

I felt proud to introduce him as my boyfriend when we ran into my friend Pam one night in a Monterey bar. She seemed genuinely pleased to see me again, and we renewed a friendship that included a barroom rendezvous once or twice a week.

I liked Pam's wild and unpredictable personality. She could drink almost as much as I could and always seemed to have a connection for a smorgasbord of drugs. And while I stuck to my vow to never again mess with LSD, I did try speed and liked the rush I got from it.

So my new image was pretty much a nine-to-five facade. My private life was far from the conservative, professional picture I tried to paint for Mrs. Felton, or for my aunt and uncle. Not one of them ever gave any indication that they suspected the truth.

Until the night I almost blew everything.

I had stopped at a friend's after work and drunk some wine. Then I remembered I'd promised to meet Pam at Tia Maria's, a bar down on Monterey's Fishermen's Wharf. But on the drive across town, I began to feel so nauseous that I decided to head back to Aunt Martha's and go to bed. So I took the shortcut home.

I'd had enough to drink so that everything looked a little blurry, but I was having no serious trouble driving until everything went black. My car crossed the boulevard into the oncoming lane and smashed head-on into a parked vehicle on the far side of the street.

When the sirens awakened me, I didn't know where I was or what had happened. People were screaming. Blood covered the front of my jacket. Paramedics pulled me out of my car, lifted me onto a stretcher, and loaded me into an ambulance for a fast trip to the hospital.

I was lucky. Though my new car was a wreck, I received only a few minor bruises and a severely cut lip.

I was just as lucky on another score: The police who were following the ambulance to the hospital to get my statement received another emergency call. So by the time the doctor in the emergency room came to release me and send me home, the police still hadn't arrived.

I didn't want to call my aunt and uncle and have them learn I'd been driving and drinking and had a wreck. So I called a friend from work—an older woman named Rose—who picked me up within minutes and drove me to her house. When the police finally located me to fill out their report so much time had passed that there was no point in a breathalyzer test. All they could do was cite me for reckless driving—a charge that carried a five-dollar fine.

When the police walked out the door a flood of relief washed over me. What followed immediately was a tidal wave of embarrassment—and guilt. *What will I tell my aunt and uncle? Worse yet, what am I going to say to Mrs. Felton? She's been so good to me. She worked it out so I could buy my car with no credit rating.*

I simply lied to my aunt. I told her I had been in an accident, that it had been the other person's fault, and that I was going to stay at my friend's for the night. I ended up staying there for two weeks and never actually living with Aunt Martha and Uncle Tim again. I'd been embarrassed by my wreck, and I didn't ever want them to find out.

Mrs. Felton was a different story. I had to call her the next morning to say I'd been in an accident and wouldn't be coming into work that day. Incredibly, she never asked for any details. She just told me she was happy I was going to be okay and to take care of myself until I could return. No lectures. No interrogation. Yet she must have suspected something.

Rose suggested that maybe I needed to cut down on my

drinking, and I had to admit it might be a good idea. Determined never to let anything like this happen again, I decided I'd have to rebuild any trust I'd lost with Mrs. Felton by working even harder on the job and cleaning up my life outside the office. The first part was easy. The second proved more difficult.

For a week I didn't touch a drop of alcohol. But when my cuts and bruises healed and I went back to work, I began drinking again and was soon consuming as much or more than before.

I got my car fixed at the dealership with my insurance claim money. The mechanics recommended I sell it, so I did. I paid off the remainder of my loan and took out another loan to buy a small used car.

I stayed with Rose for a while, paying only nominal rent but trying to reciprocate by doing all the housekeeping and a lot of the cooking for her. Finally, Rose and I worked out a more permanent arrangement. She enjoyed having a roommate and I couldn't afford to live alone. Rose wasn't the kind of person I had looked for as a roommate. She was as close to my mom's age as she was to mine. But I think I saw the quiet stability of her lifestyle as an anchor that could keep my own life under control. I wanted to begin a new chapter in my life.

And by the time I'd been working at Pride Buick for six months, Mrs. Felton asked me if I'd be interested in taking some management training classes. She told me she thought I had the potential to take over her job as business manager in three or four years if I was willing to work for it.

The promise of success never seemed brighter. I could almost see the victory that I'd been searching for for so long.

CHAPTER 10

SEARCHING FOR LOVE

*E*very morning, just before work, I'd greet John in the company lunchroom with a kiss. We'd sit down and have a quick cup of coffee together. At break time he'd come by my desk to say hi, and at lunch we'd go off by ourselves. Our office romance seemed so convenient, so perfect.

Except for one hitch. Mrs. Felton didn't approve of John. She didn't come right out and say so, but one day she told me in a rather motherly tone, "You really ought to date around more, Becky. You're young, and you don't want to get tied down to one person before you really know what you're looking for."

If my own mother had said that, I'd have blown up and told her to mind her own business. But I didn't react that way to Mrs. Felton because I knew she really liked me and wanted what was best for me. Basically she didn't think John was good enough for me. So even though I didn't heed her advice, I did listen and thought about what she said.

The trouble is, I thought, *she doesn't really know John well enough to see all his good points. And she doesn't know me well enough to know I'm not as wonderful as she thinks.*

Yet I worked hard to try to live up to Mrs. Felton's expectations. Before long I not only mastered all the parts of my expanded job, I learned the routine for the used car desk, the new car desk, and even passed the required tests to become a Notary Public for the State of California.

In the meantime, my romantic road turned rocky when the car business took a slump. The dealership let several employees go, and John was one of them. I halfway suspected Mrs. Felton had something to say about who got a pink slip, but that didn't make me any less determined to prove myself to her.

Without the constant contact fueling our relationship, John and I began to have more conflicts. We no longer shared the biggest part of our lives, and I sensed us slowly drifting apart. When I accused John of not caring as much for me as he had before, we would get into a big fight. Sometimes we'd go a week or two before making up.

The emotional roller coaster eventually ran its course. And when I heard John's high school girlfriend was back in the picture, I decided to give him an ultimatum; her or me.

I was afraid I knew what his decision would be, so I made my own decision. I would break up with him before he had a chance to dump me. That way it would be my decision, not his.

I decided to break the news to John at the party my roommate was planning to give at our apartment for my twenty-first birthday. What better time than the day I came of age to get a brand new start.

We expected a good turnout—December is always a good month for parties. A lot of single people lived in our apartment complex, and Rose had invited a big group from the dealership. However, I'd never imagined the size of the crowd that showed up. And I know Rose was surprised, too. By nine o'clock in the evening more than fifty guests were crammed into our little apartment—drinking, dancing, talking—and drinking.

John stood beside me, smiling and talking as I greeted my friends and accepted my gifts—most of which seemed to be bottles of wine, cartons of cigarettes, or fifths of hard liquor. I was, after all, twenty-one, and of legal age now. After all those years of pretending, of forging IDs, I'd finally made it to twenty-one.

I deserved to celebrate—and I did! It felt like New Year's Eve. More friends than I ever knew I had were there to celebrate with me.

Some time into the evening, Pam, my wild friend from my

old job, showed up. She'd invited four older guys who lived in the apartment next to hers. I'd met them once when I'd been over to her place. This night, though, as soon as they walked in I noticed how incredibly good-looking one of them was. Ironically, his name was also John. Tall, blond, and muscular, he was also tanned from working as a construction worker and being an avid outdoorsman. The minute he walked into my apartment I knew he was the best-looking guy I had ever seen, and he wasn't there five minutes before I asked him to dance.

I never did tell the old John we were through. I didn't have to. He left the party early, and the new John stayed.

What a party! What a day! What a night! I'd become an adult—and I'd fallen in love.

This John was different from anyone I'd ever gone out with. He was strong—not just physically—but he was a strong person. He was fun-loving and handsome, but he was stable, too. He owned property and was responsible for a construction crew. He was four years older than I, but it wasn't just his age that made him seem so mature. The guys I had dated before were boys. John was a man.

Always before I had held back with guys. I always tried not to care too much for fear of being hurt. This time it was different. Within a week I knew John was the "forever" guy I had been waiting for. He was someone I could commit myself to, someone strong enough to trust with my weakness and my love. But that little tinge of fear was still there, the fear of rejection—the fear that he didn't care about me as much as I cared about him. So I didn't tell him I'd decided he was the one I was going to marry. However, I did decide to do whatever it took to make him feel the same way about me.

A lot happened in the three weeks between my birthday party and Christmas. My mature, stable roommate decided to move out of town, and I arranged to move in with Pam. Once again I found myself with a wonderfully convenient romance—this time with my next-door neighbor. Except for my time at work, we were together almost constantly.

John went away on a previously planned trip with friends at Christmas, and Pam left to spend the holidays with family. And so I found myself alone on Christmas Eve, and on Christmas morning I awakened in utter solitude to an empty apartment.

An hour or so after I woke up, I wandered out to the living room and sat by myself on the couch to open the Christmas package my parents had sent me—another robe.

I held the robe on my lap and thought back to my first California Christmas with Tina. I wondered what kind of holiday she was having in Alaska, if she was still there. Maybe she was back in Illinois now. The thought made me feel lonelier and farther from Illinois than I'd ever felt before.

I ate Christmas dinner with Aunt Martha and Uncle Tim, but their hospitality did little to counter the emptiness. Afterwards I tried to fill the aching hole by visiting some of the people I worked with to deliver the wooden, decoupaged Christmas cards I'd made for them.

At each stop I was welcomed like a lost relative and served wine or champagne. So by the time I stopped for my last delivery at Mrs. Felton's house, I'd lost count of the stops—and the drinks I'd downed.

Mrs. Felton greeted me warmly and invited me in to meet her family. When I presented her with the card I had made for her, she seemed genuinely touched. I could tell, though, from the concerned look on her face as she listened to me talk that she knew I was drunk; I must have been slurring my words.

She asked me to stay, but I insisted that I had to be going. "But how will you get home?" she wanted to know, obviously concerned about my driving.

"I'll be okay," I said. It wasn't until an hour later, as I finally got away from her house, that I realized she'd been deliberately stalling me. And that she hadn't offered me anything to drink.

The worst of the loneliness left when Pam and John got back, but the intense dissatisfaction I'd experienced over Christmas forced me to face the fact that something was still missing in my life. Maybe that's why I decided to stop again one day at that church. Not that I really expected that minister to help me. But then he had helped me before, and I'd never properly thanked him for his encouragement.

I wondered if he'd even remember me, but he did. He acted genuinely pleased to learn I'd stayed in the area and taken the job at the dealership. I filled him in on my new job and Tina's trip to Alaska. I didn't feel comfortable talking about my loneliness or my relationship with John, so I quickly ran out of things to say. As a passing thought, as much to fill the increasing gaps in the conversation as anything else, I asked if the church ever needed help with its youth group.

To my surprise and sudden uneasiness, the pastor replied, "As a matter of fact, we could use some help. If you're interested, you could meet the man who teaches our high school Sunday school class right now. Ralph doubles as the church janitor. I think you'll like him."

Wishing I could graciously leave, I instead followed the pastor out of his office. We found Ralph in the church basement. He was dressed in a red flannel shirt, blue jeans, and work boots; his reddish-blond hair and beard made him look older than his thirty years.

He wasn't at all what I'd expected, but when he grinned and greeted me, I felt like I'd known him for a long time. As we talked the only thing that made me uncomfortable was the way Ralph talked about God—using the name "Jesus" as if he was some everyday friend. Ralph even recited a couple of verses from the Bible, right in the middle of our conversation.

"Be glad for you to join us this Sunday if you can make it," he said as I said good-bye. I promised to be there.

For some reason, I kept my promise—partly because I knew something was missing in my life, and partly because I knew I needed to make a fresh start. So I went to church the next Sunday believing, or at least hoping, it could make a difference.

But the doubts descended on me the moment I walked

into Ralph's Sunday school classroom and heard him exclaim, "Welcome, Sister!"

Whoa! This is weird, I thought. And that opinion seemed confirmed during Sunday school when he wandered off on a tangent and began warning the kids in the class about the dangers of Ouija boards. Everyone I knew had played with Ouija boards at one time or another. They seemed pretty harmless to me, hardly deserving of the kind of dire warning about satanic power Ralph delivered.

Yet I realized that first Sunday in his class that Ralph knew a lot more about God and the Bible than anyone else I knew. And although I went a second Sunday, I quickly discarded any thought of trying to help Ralph out with his class.

I also realized I wasn't living up to the standards of conduct Ralph talked about in his lessons. So, telling myself I didn't want to be a hypocrite, but mostly because I felt uneasy around Ralph, I decided to forget church altogether.

It seemed just as well. My relationship with John, which grew more serious by the week, proved an effective antidote to the loneliness I'd felt at Christmas.

Yet I couldn't seem to get away from this Ralph. I occasionally saw him around town, and he would wave and hurry over to talk—usually about God. "Have you been reading your Bible, Becky?" he always wanted to know.

I would mumble some excuse and he would say, "You really need to be reading the Word. Start in the New Testament. Read the book of John. You'll find a lot of help for . . ."

About that time I'd apologize and make up some reason why I had to be going and hurry away as fast as I could. A couple of times, after encounters with Ralph, I pulled out the old Bible I'd gotten during my confirmation classes and tried to read a little. But it didn't seem very relevant to me. For Ralph maybe. I decided if Ralph expected me to get anything out of the Bible, he was expecting too much.

Some days I thought Mrs. Felton also expected too much from me. But it never seemed to bother me coming from her. Like the time she walked into the break room as I stubbed out a cigarette. "You really ought to quit smoking, Becky," she said. "You'd be a lot healthier."

"I know," I admitted. "I've been thinking about quitting."

"Why don't you then? Maybe I can make it worth your while. What would it take to motivate you? What could I give you as a reward?"

What started as a casual conversation quickly turned serious as I realized she really did want to do something to help. I tried to tell her she didn't need to do anything for me, but she wasn't about to back off. We finally agreed on an incentive. She owned a gorgeous red convertible she seldom took out of her garage. She knew I had admired the car on several occasions, so she made me an offer. A month after I gave up smoking completely, she would let me have the keys to the convertible for two weeks.

Thirty days after our conversation, she lived up to her promise—and I had kicked my nicotine habit.

But my drinking was another story.

For one reason, I was even more concerned about pleasing John than pleasing Mrs. Felton, and drinking was a big part of what we did together. We would meet for a few drinks after work. With dinner, we would have wine or beer. Sometimes there was an after-dinner drink. And most nights, before going to bed, we would snuggle into a big chair in front of his fireplace and sip Cold Duck as the crackling fire slowly changed to glowing embers. On weekends when we went hiking or canoeing or just lay on the beach, we always took a supply of beer.

As the weeks rolled by, I felt more convinced than ever that John was my fairy-tale prince. In all my previous relationships, I'd been the spontaneous one, the instigator, the leader. I didn't have to do that with John. He took charge and I just enjoyed being swept along.

I never knew what to expect. Any night after work he might be waiting for me with a picnic basket all packed. We would take a two-hour drive to Big Sur and eat a romantic supper seated on a blanket high on a bluff as we watched the sun set over the Pacific. Or he'd throw a couple of sleeping bags and a tent in the back of his pickup and announce, "We're going to sleep tonight under a redwood tree," and we'd be off for the weekend to the mountains.

One night just about the time the sun began to set, we were walking out of Tia Maria's when John said, "It's such a nice night, I've got an idea." The next thing I knew he had borrowed a two-man raft from someone on the pier, and we were paddling out into Monterey Bay. After we had gotten away from shore, we stopped paddling and just sat there watching the sun set and listening to the gulls squawking overhead.

Suddenly I heard a strange noise so close it made me start. *Arghf! Arghf!* I quickly looked over the edge of the raft to see a huge dark body swimming toward us. My heart did a flip-flop as I heard an answering *arghf* coming toward us from the other side.

"John!" I screamed. "What is it?"

Seeing how frightened I was, John burst into laughter. "It's okay, Becky. They're not going to hurt us. They're just curious. See?"

I looked where he was pointing to see, just a few feet from our raft, the silly mustached face of a huge walrus. I had to laugh. I suddenly was aware that I felt very secure to be there with John. I'd never known anyone like him—and I never wanted anyone else.

I thought he felt the same way about me. Until one spring morning when he announced he was going down to Los Angeles for the weekend to visit an old college girlfriend.

"You're what?" I asked incredulously.

"I haven't seen her in a long time," he said. "She invited me down, and I figured it'd be a good chance to get caught up. See some friends in LA . . ."

There was just one fact I wanted to know. "And where are you planning on staying while you're there?"

"At her apartment, I guess," he replied.

"Wonderful!" I said, my voice choked with emotion as I reeled from the blow of this revelation.

"I'm taking my sleeping bag so I can sack out on her living room floor," John said. "I don't think I'll be sleeping with her, if that's what's bothering you."

"You 'don't think'?" Now I was mad. "You're leaving me here by myself while you go off to spend the weekend with an old girlfriend. And I'm supposed to feel okay about it because you're taking a sleeping bag and you *don't think* you'll sleep with her?

"Don't I mean anything to you? Haven't these last few months meant anything to you? I love you!"

"I love him!" I told Mrs. Felton when she called me into her office, closed the door, and asked what was bothering me. I told her about John's LA trip plans.

Mrs. Felton listened and then gently said, "Maybe he's using you, Becky. Perhaps you'd be better off without him."

"No!" I couldn't think of that. "I love him—and he loves me."

"Has he asked you to marry him?"

"No," I said, "but that's because he's just not ready to get married. He's not even sure he believes in marriage. But I know he loves me."

"I thought you loved me," I said to John that night.

"I do," he replied.

"Then how can you think of spending the weekend with someone else? How can you even consider the remote possibility of sleeping with her?"

"You're overreacting, Becky," he said. "It's just a chance to visit an old friend. It doesn't mean anything."

"Well, it does to me," I said. "I love you. And because I love you I would never think of spending the weekend with someone else. I would never dream of being with anyone else, of sleeping with anyone else. And if you care anything at all about me, you won't go."

"I do care," he insisted. But he went anyway.

And while he was gone, I went to San Francisco to party for the weekend with friends. They had some cocaine, which

I had never tried before. I figured, "What's there to lose?" and did my first coke. I was still so high the next morning that I went out by myself for a cup of coffee and couldn't find my way back to the apartment where we were staying. I got confused because everything seemed so vague that I made a wrong turn at one point only to find myself driving the wrong way down an interstate. After what seemed like hours driving up and down unfamiliar streets, my friends spotted me and ran out of the apartment to flag me down. We all laughed, but I decided then that cocaine wasn't for me. I'd never been that out of control with booze. Coke scared me.

I didn't tell John about my weekend, and he didn't talk about his. I took him back, and our relationship went on much as it had before, except that I now felt more possessive than ever. When I wasn't with John, I wondered where he was and who he was with. I dieted to lose weight and make myself more attractive to him, and I jealously worried whenever I saw him looking in any other girl's direction. I constantly told him I loved him and asked him to share his feelings for me. But the words couldn't dispel my growing doubts and fears.

When he broke the news that he planned to be gone to Canada for a two-month wilderness camping trip, I just knew I would lose him. He'd meet some other girl and that would be the end for us.

John laughed when I confronted him with my fears. He told me he'd been going on these annual trips for years, and if past experience held true, he wouldn't even lay eyes on another girl the entire time he and his buddies were in the north woods. I remained unconvinced and began to live in dread of the July day he planned to leave.

My only consolation came late that spring in the form of a letter postmarked, "Chicago, Illinois." I tore it open to find a letter from my old friend Penny, saying our high-school graduating class was planning our five-year reunion in July—a whole year early. It sounded crazy, but fun. And John was going to be gone anyway. So I checked with Mrs. Felton to make sure I could get a week off. Then I made my plane reservations for the same date John had set to leave for Canada and wrote to tell Penny and my parents I'd be coming home.

After two years, I was finally going home with a feeling of pride. I could hardly wait. I had pictures of John I could show to impress my friends, and work was going great. My high school days had never seemed to gain me the important status symbols I had now.

But while my professional life soared, my personal life dragged bottom. Weeks of jealousy and worry about John were taking their toll. Drinking seemed the only thing that eased my mind, so I drank more than ever. I would go to bed high every night and feel so low when I awakened that I would pop a hit or two of speed to get me going. I didn't feel very good depending so much on drugs, but the amphetamines worked so well I began taking them throughout the day. I discovered that six or eight hits a day gave me more than enough energy to do my job and do it well.

Neither the drinking nor the drugs, though, could completely allay my fears of losing John, nor could they put off the day of our parting.

John drove me to the airport in his pickup, which was already packed with his fishing gear and his other camping supplies. From the airport he was heading on to Canada.

I cried at the gate, clinging to his arm and sobbing, "It's n-n-never going to be b-b-better than I am."

"Come on," he said. "There's not going to be anyone else in Canada." But nothing he said would console me.

"I love you," I sobbed. "And even if *you're* not ready to make a commitment, I am. I'm going to be faithful to you no matter what!"

With that declaration of my loyalty, I kissed him good-bye. But as I walked up the jetway and onto my plane, I couldn't shake the feeling that when he came back from Canada our relationship would be forever changed.

I was right about that. But I couldn't have been more wrong about the reason.

CHAPTER 11

"I THINK I'M AN ALCOHOLIC!"

When the flight attendants started taking drink orders I realized this was my first flight since I'd turned twenty-one. I could have whatever I wanted and no one could stop me.

"Scotch on the rocks," I told the woman who stopped at my seat. By the time we touched down to connect with a Denver flight I'd finished off three. I added several more empty bottles to my collection between LA and Denver and felt a lot higher than thirty thousand feet.

The plan called for me to meet an old college friend named Vicki in Denver, and we'd spend the night seeing the city. The next day I'd fly up to Wisconsin to visit my sister, where my folks were also going to be visiting for the weekend.

Fortunately I wasn't too drunk when we landed to recognize my name being paged. I found one of the white courtesy phones and called the main desk. The message was for me to call Vicki at one of the airline desks.

"Sorry," she said when I reached her, "It's only one o'clock here, and I can't get off this shift until three. Why don't you wait for me in the airport bar?"

By the time she found me, I was totally wasted. She drove me to her apartment where she changed for the evening, and we drove downtown looking for action. About the time we walked into the first bar, I'd begun to sober up again.

I have no idea how many bars we went to or how many people we danced with. When it came time to go home, neither of us was in any shape to drive. But I poured Vicki into the passenger seat and slipped behind the wheel.

"Which way?" I asked.

"Which way what?" Vicki responded.

"To home. How do we get home?"

Vicki sat up slowly and looked out the front windshield. "I thinksh that'sh the way," she slurred, pointing behind us.

"Okay," I responded, pulling out into the street and bouncing over the median as we made an illegal U-turn. Somehow we made it back to Vicki's place.

And somehow we got to the airport the next morning in time for me to catch my flight to Madison to meet my family. Nearly two years had passed since I'd seen any of them, and I was excited to tell them all about my job and John.

Mom and Dad hugged me the moment I came through the gate. But the warm greetings didn't disguise the disappointment in my mother's eyes as she realized how hung over I was. Even before she had a chance to say anything, I thought, *Here we go again. Nothing between us has changed.*

I talked most of the weekend—mostly to prevent my parents from lecturing me and to keep the conversation on "safe" subjects. I told every detail I could think of about my job and the people I worked with, including Mrs. Felton. I proudly told my family I'd quit smoking, and I talked some about John. I wasn't totally candid about our relationship, of course, but I dropped a few hints that I was serious about him and that he was the one I wanted to marry.

I couldn't wait for the weekend to end so I could get on another plane and fly on to Chicago. My folks planned to drive and weren't going to be home before Tuesday. I'd be home alone with no one but my friends to worry about.

Practically the whole gang met me at the airport, and we headed off to Faces, our favorite community bar, to celebrate before I even had time to unpack my bags. I got so drunk I had everybody laughing and exclaiming how great it was to have me back. Time and again I heard one friend or another exclaim, "Same old Becky." It felt good to be accepted.

The surprise I got on Tuesday made me feel even better. Just as I walked out of the house to meet my friends, a familiar-looking pickup pulled slowly into the drive. I looked twice and still didn't believe it.

"John!" I shouted as I went racing across the yard and threw my arms around the man I'd feared I'd never see again. After a long, passionate embrace, I finally let go and gasped, "What are you doing here?"

He grinned. "I was on my way to Canada. I looked at a map and suddenly realized Chicago is just down the lake from there."

"But wasn't it a little out of your way?" I said, laughing.

"Only a few hundred miles. And it was worth the drive just to see you again."

I hugged him again and tried to fight back the tears of happiness.

John only stayed a day, but he got to meet my folks and I had a chance to show him off to all my friends.

I felt wonderfully loved and reassured by his visit—to think he had driven so far knowing how much it would mean to me. So our Illinois good-bye left me feeling a lot more hopeful than the airport scene in California. He hadn't made any promises of a long-term commitment, but I took his visit as a hopeful sign. It gave me even more reason to renew my vow of love and faithfulness. I knew John was the man, the only man, for me.

Wednesday night I went out drinking once again. Thursday night I was invited to a big party.

One of my friends and I had finished off a fifth of vodka between us before seven o'clock. Then we talked everyone into heading down to Faces for more.

There I ran into George, an old party acquaintance from high school who'd gone to college at Illinois State University. We danced together for a while and had a few more drinks before someone suggested we all drive out to the local rock quarry and go skinny-dipping. I didn't feel like it, but if everyone else went, I figured I'd go along. Before we left, I ordered one more drink. And that was the last thing I remembered until . . . My head was pounding as I opened my eyes just enough to see the red numbers of a clock—5:03! But it wasn't my clock.

A split second later I was fully awake. *Where am I?* I didn't recognize the room. I rolled over and froze when I felt someone beside me. *Who's that?*

For an instant I didn't recognize him in the predawn darkness. Then I knew. *George! But what am I doing with . . .*

I suddenly felt nauseous. I frantically tried to remember how I had gotten there. *What had happened the night before? What had I done?* I racked my brain, but I remembered nothing.

My next thoughts were of John. I had promised him I would be loyal no matter what, and in less than two days since he left for Canada this happened! *But exactly what did happen?* I still couldn't remember a thing. To make matters worse I had no idea where I was, what street I was on, or even where I had left my car. I had to wait until my "friend" woke up to ask him for a ride home.

I rode the entire way in humiliated silence, desperately trying to recall something, anything, from the night before.

My embarrassment and the horrible, sick feeling in the pit of my stomach kept me from asking what had happened. I could only imagine. I asked myself over and over and over, *How? How? How?* There was only one possible explanation. *I've lost total control of who I am.*

I suddenly knew what my problem really was. There was no denying it.

I trudged up the front steps and slipped into the house. The big clock in the living room said it was a little after six. The next thing my bleary eyes focused on was my mother, lying on the couch, where she had obviously fallen asleep waiting for me to get home the night before. She stirred as I tried to gently close the front door. "Becky?" She sat up and looked right at me.

I expected her to interrogate me. To explode. To do something. But she just sat there. Maybe she could tell by looking at me that she didn't need to say anything. Nothing she could have said would have made me feel any worse, any lower, or any more ashamed.

Neither of us spoke as I walked over to an easy chair facing the couch and sat down. Finally, after another eternal silence, I blurted out the conclusion I'd come to in the car on the way home: "Oh, Mom. I think I'm an alcoholic."

I had never said that before—never even thought it before that morning. But I knew it was true—and so did Mom.

We both began to cry, and I rushed across the room and fell into her arms.

I sobbed so uncontrollably I couldn't get any words out, but the thoughts tumbled over one another in my mind. *What am I going to do? How could I let this happen? Why didn't I see it before? What happens next?*

All I could do was cry and think, *I'm only twenty-one years old! What have I done to myself?* Finally I regained enough control to tell my mom I had to go to bed. There I curled up under the covers—wishing I never had to get up, wishing I'd never come home, wishing none of this had happened, wishing I were dead!

But I *wasn't* dead and it *had* happened. I had come home, and soon I would have to get up and go to the class reunion that night where all my friends expected me to be "the same old Becky." I would rather have been anyone else.

I stayed in bed most of the morning asking myself, *What am I going to do now?* When I finally got up, what I did was pretend. I decided I simply wouldn't drink that night. I'd just pretend nothing was wrong.

It wasn't easy. Driving to the reunion, Penny offered me a drink. When I declined, she asked, "Why not?"

"I just don't feel like drinking tonight."

She looked puzzled. "What's wrong?"

"Nothing," I insisted. But I could tell she didn't believe me.

I made it through the first couple of hours by moving around and greeting all the people I recognized, whether or not I could think of their names. But I desperately wanted a drink.

Finally, I slipped into the bathroom just off the dance hall, wanting to be alone for a moment as well as check my hair and my makeup. But I wasn't alone. There, looking in the mirror, was Penny.

"How's it going?" she asked.

"Perfect," I assured her.

She met my eyes in the mirror before she asked, "Are you really not gonna drink tonight?"

I shook my head. "No."

"But Becky," she said, her voice prodding as much as her words, "Why not? You're the life of the party when you do."

"I just can't," I responded sadly, *really* wishing I could drink. I walked out of the women's room feeling terribly torn; I didn't want to have to explain my problems to my friends, but I so badly wanted someone to understand.

I did slip outside and smoke some dope so I could be high and loose for the rest of the evening, but I didn't drink a drop, despite my friends' goading me to "go for it" and "get rowdy."

When my plane lifted off for California the next day, I had been dry for three days. Mom didn't want me to go, but I knew Mrs. Felton expected me on Monday morning and I couldn't let her down. I didn't want to add any more to my guilt.

As the plane winged westward I thought of the mess I'd made of my life and how I'd betrayed the man I loved. I tried to imagine how I would make my confession to John. I knew I'd have to tell him; I didn't want any secrets between us. But I didn't want to write him, and I couldn't call him in the Canadian wilderness.

I'll just have to wait until he gets back, I told myself. But I didn't think I could bear to live with the guilt for two whole months.

Pam had promised to meet my plane in Monterey, but she wasn't at the gate. I picked up my luggage but she wasn't in the baggage area either. I called our apartment. No answer. So I waited. After an hour I called Aunt Martha and Uncle Tim, who came and drove me to my apartment.

No Pam. I had been a little irritated at first. Now I began to worry.

With my body still on Central time and my emotions frayed after three and a half days without a drink, I went to bed. I don't know what time it was when I heard the apartment door slam shut.

"Pam?" I called. And I heard her bump into something in the living room before she started down the hall. Finally her silhouette appeared in my doorway.

"Becky, you're home!" She sounded surprised. "I'm sorry, I forgot you were coming."

"Can you come in a minute? I need to talk."

Pam walked in and took a seat on the edge of my bed. "What's up, Beck?"

I took a deep breath. I had to tell someone. "Pam, I want you to know that I think I'm an alcoholic."

"No," she laughed.

"I think I am."

"You are not. You gotta be kidding!"

"I'm serious, Pam."

"No way are you an alcoholic. Why don't you just get some sleep? You'll feel better in the morning."

I couldn't sleep. I don't know what I'd expected. Concern? Support? All I'd gotten from Pam was denial. I knew I'd already had enough of that.

I didn't feel any better the next morning. My spirits and my body were dragging so bad that the first thing I did after dressing for work was to walk to visit my neighbor. Sam was everyone's favorite connection. "I need some speed," I told him. He sold the stuff in little bags with a hundred pills in them.

"Sorry, Beck," he said. "I'm fresh out."

"I've got to get some."

"Maybe I'll make a connection by the end of the week."

I didn't think I could survive straight till the end of the week. After a few more days of drinking only diet soft drinks, I felt as if my life was coming unglued. I cried

"I THINK I'M AN ALCOHOLIC!"

uncontrollably. I sweated and itched. Sometimes I felt as if little ants were crawling around on my scalp.

I went back to Sam two days later, but he still didn't have anything. "And I don't even know when I'll be getting another supply," he informed me.

Pam invited me to go down to Morro Bay for the weekend to visit some friends. I had to do something so I said yes. The first thing we did when we got there was to head out to a bar, where Pam ordered me a drink and insisted I have "just one." Next thing I knew it was morning, and I had the sickest hangover in history.

I let Pam know how angry I was, but what I didn't even try to communicate was my sad feeling of betrayal and the terrifying realization that I was all alone in my struggle.

For a while I kept going to parties, showing up carrying a six-pack of Dr. Pepper. The second I finished off the can in my hand, I'd pop open another. But having something to sip and something to do with my hands didn't do a thing to loosen me up. And my friends noticed. "You're taking this too seriously, Becky," they'd say. "You need to relax and not overdo this. Maybe cut back a little at a time."

They didn't understand. I couldn't cut back. If I drank at all, I drank until I got drunk. I soon avoided the pressure and my friends by staying home by myself. But that gave me more time than I wanted to think—about my problems, about John. I spent hours writing and rewriting my confession to him before I'd tear up the paper in frustration and guilt. Perhaps my alcoholism explained why I did what I did, but it was no excuse.

One night, at home alone, I locked myself in my room without food or drink because I couldn't bring myself to open the refrigerator and see the half-empty bottle of wine I knew was there. Hunger finally forced me from my hideout and into the living room. I walked past Pam's old cat, sleeping on the corner of the sofa. The cat had recently contracted a bad case of fleas, and as I passed by, suddenly I thought I felt something jumping around my feet. In fact, I felt as if fleas were crawling and jumping all over me.

I completely lost control and began to scream. Then I thought they were in my mind, just like crazy thoughts—jumping and twisting and tormenting me, until I fled crying back to my room, where I eventually regained my composure. But by then I felt certain I was going crazy.

One person who tried to help was my mom. Again and again she called, trying to convince me to go to Alcoholic's Anonymous or somewhere else for help. Finally after she called and begged for three days in a row, I promised her I'd give it a try. I checked a local paper and learned there was a local AA chapter especially for young people. So that's where I went.

Just getting out of the car seemed like the hardest thing I'd ever done. I had to force one foot ahead of the other as I walked up the sidewalk to a stone cottage overlooking the Pacific Ocean.

The session had already started when I slipped into the back of a rustic meeting room illuminated only by the light of the sunset outside and a blazing stack of logs in a stone fireplace. The smell of coffee and wood smoke gave the place a homey, peaceful air; it was a complete contrast to the stormy turmoil raging inside me.

Looking around curiously, I noted a number of young faces. Some looked familiar enough to make me wonder if I'd seen them, maybe even partied with them at one of the local night spots.

They seemed to be going around the room, taking turns talking, introducing themselves and telling a bit of their own stories. Each person, by way of introduction, would begin by giving his or her first name and saying, "I'm an alcoholic." This admission seemed to be a requirement of anyone who wished to talk.

As I listened to all the confessions, all the stories, tears ran down my face. Embarrassed, I tried to wipe them away, but no one seemed to notice.

Finally, after the woman next to me had introduced herself, I slowly rose to my feet and said, "I'm Becky, and I'm an alcoholic." I might have said more, but I was crying too hard—crying with shame and embarrassment for having to stand up in front of a group of complete strangers and admit what I had become. When I sat down again, someone else stood up and the attention shifted away from me.

Once the introductions were over, a middle-aged man stood up at the front of the room. Evidently a special speaker for the evening, he began by saying, "Hi, I'm Pete. And I've been an alcoholic for twenty years...."

"I've been an alcoholic for twenty years...." The rock walls echoed those words and sent them reverberating through my mind, again and again. Each time the words were amplified, louder and louder until I could hear nothing but those words. *Twenty years? Twenty years. Twenty years! I can't do this, I can't come here for twenty years! I won't! I'd rather die!*

The tears returned once more, but this time they were tears of hopelessness and despair. AA wasn't going to be the answer for me. I knew that.

I tried to slip out the back as soon as the meeting concluded, but a young man in his early twenties cut me off and introduced himself. His name was Bill. He told me he was a soldier stationed at Fort Ord and he was in an alcohol rehabilitation program at the base hospital. As part of his treatment they kept him in a locked ward every night and put him on a drug called antibuse. If he took so much as a sip of alcohol, its reaction with the drug would make him so violently sick he'd wish he could die.

I'm sure Bill just wanted to be friendly and encouraging, but he succeeded only in deepening my despair. *If the only solutions to alcoholism are AA or antibuse,* I thought, *I wish I could die now.*

In the desperate days following my visit to AA, something made me think of Ralph, the youth worker. Figuring I had nothing to lose, I went to see him at the church.

He didn't act at all surprised that I'd looked him up. When I told him I had a drinking problem, he told me I needed to take my troubles to God. He said Jesus wanted to be my friend if I'd let him, but I couldn't believe God or anyone else could love me the way I was. I had to change first—and I didn't know how to change.

When I left Ralph, I felt more depressed than ever. Not even God could help me.

As a last resort, I went to the last person in the world I wanted to know about my problem. I walked into Mrs. Felton's office, sat down in a chair in front of her desk, and began to cry. In between sobs I finally forced out the words: "I think I have a drinking problem."

She remained quiet for a few moments, never registering any surprise. "Are you getting some help, Becky?" she wanted to know.

I told her I had been talking to someone at church and had been to one AA meeting. She told me she thought those were good steps to take and she was glad I was trying to get help. She said she felt that was a good sign.

"Let me know if there's anything I can do to help," she added. I knew she meant it and was heartened by her nonjudgmental acceptance and support, but in that instant I also knew she didn't know how to help. Since I didn't have the foggiest idea what to ask of her, I walked out of her office, more disheartened than ever to realize I still needed help and there was nowhere else to turn.

CHAPTER 12

ONE REAL VICTORY

*I*n the following days and weeks, my first without alcohol or drugs in years, I felt as if the world were tightening on me like a vise. I moved slowly, painfully through my daily routines, afraid I would crack. As the pressure mounted, my life seemed ready to explode.

The fuse was finally lit when I received a summons to a formal deposition on the automobile wreck I had been involved in over a year before. The case had taken so long I had nearly forgotten about it. Now on top of all the other pressures the wheels of justice began to grind. My recorded testimony would be the first step in deciding whether or not the case, a civil suit filed by the owner of the other car, would go to court. And I was scared.

The letter came to me at the office, on insurance company letterhead, instructing me where to go for the deposition. I showed the letter to Mrs. Felton, who assured me I could have half a day off and that the entire matter looked very routine. I wasn't so sure.

I literally trembled with tension on the drive to Watsonville, the county seat. As I headed north along the ocean, I mentally reviewed my life—the drinking, all the stupid times I'd been drunk, the accident, the night of the class reunion party in Chicago—and admitted I was out of control. I also thought about the past weeks since I had given up drinking, given up speed, and begun to cut back on marijuana. I felt a tinge of hope I was almost afraid to acknowledge. I wanted to change. I had been trying to change.

As I thought about all this, I decided I would take yet

another step toward cleaning up my life. I decided I would stop deceiving people—I'd tell the truth about the accident. If I was ready to face the truth about myself, I wasn't going to lie to others either.

I felt my determination wavering as I parked my car outside an old California-style building and walked slowly up the walk. Inside I presented myself to a receptionist, who directed me down a long hall. I stopped in front of two huge wooden doors with the name of my insurance company's law firm engraved on a heavy metal plaque.

The moment I entered, a man in a three-piece suit approached me and inquired, "Rebecca?" I knew by the official tone of his voice I was in for serious trouble.

"Come with me," he instructed, leading me into his office and directing me to a seat in front of his expansive mahogany desk. He looked at me for a few moments before he said, "I'm going to take you to another office in a few minutes, but I wanted to talk to you before the deposition to make sure you understand the seriousness of this." I noted a steely hard look in his eyes as he continued, "This deposition is very official. There will be a court reporter there taking down everything you say.

"Rebecca, you better tell the truth, because if you lie and this case goes to trial, and they find out you lied, you will be crucified in court and . . ."

The man kept talking, but I didn't hear anything else he said. That seldom-used word *crucified* had triggered a chain reaction in my mind. My mind flashed a picture of Jesus hanging on a cross, and suddenly everything Ralph had been trying to tell me became clear—about how Jesus' death had meaning and purpose, how he died for man's sins. I thought again about all my sins, and it hit me that Jesus died to redeem my messed-up life.

None of these flashing thoughts had time to sink in. The man finished what he was saying and quickly ushered me out of his office and down the hall to a small conference room. There we joined a representative of the other insurance company, the owner of the car I had hit, and the court reporter.

The first questions were just information. Name, address, date of birth, place of employment. Then it was established that I was indeed the driver of my car on the day of the accident at such and such a time and place. Finally, we got to the crux of the questioning.

"Had you been drinking before the accident?"

I remembered my determination to be truthful, and I thought about my lawyer's warning. "Yes."

"Where had you been drinking?"

"At a friend's house." I didn't remember the address, but I gave the name.

"How much had you drunk?"

"I don't know." That was true. I had no idea.

"Two or three drinks? More?"

"I can't remember." Again, the truth. The lawyer asked a number of related questions, but a year had passed, and I honestly couldn't remember many of the details. The things I did remember I answered truthfully.

"Were you listening to your car radio?"

"I don't remember."

"Did you fall asleep at the wheel or did you pass out?"

"I don't know what happened."

Almost an hour passed before the questioning ended and my lawyer escorted me from the room. "That's it," he said outside. "If we need anything else from you, we'll be in touch."

Whatever happened about the accident, whether it ever went to court or not, I knew I was judged guilty. Guilty of wasting the past few years. Guilty of betraying John. Guilty of tormenting my family. Guilty of alienating my friends. Guilty of making a mess of my life.

As I turned onto the Pacific Highway and headed south, the ocean almost matched the sky—California blue. The breakers stretched in ragged white chalk lines down the coast as far as I could see. And gulls looped lazily, crisscrossing the horizon.

But I didn't really see the beauty. It didn't matter—nothing mattered anymore.

As I sped along Highway 1, the majesty of the Pacific coast couldn't touch the ugliness I felt inside. Tears blurred my vision, but I didn't slow down.

Maybe I should end it all right now, I thought as the road angled upward along a cliff. *All I'd have to do is turn the wheel, sail over the edge, and plummet to the beach below. It would be so easy. Dying would be better than going on like this.*

I wanted to die. At least my parents were two thousand miles away where they couldn't see what a mess I had made of my life. I was so far from the person I wanted to be that a drop off a cliff looked like the best solution.

But I didn't turn the wheel. I couldn't. I just drove on, and without thinking, I drove right past the exit for the car dealership. When I finally realized I had missed my exit I asked myself, *Where now? There's no place left to go.*

Suddenly, I thought of Ralph. I just knew if I could find him, he'd have an answer. So I drove on for two more exits, turned off the highway, raced into the church parking lot, and screeched to a stop.

I tore into the church, ran down the steps, and stopped dead in my tracks in the basement hallway when I spotted Ralph pushing a buffing machine across a freshly waxed floor. "Oh, Ralph," I exclaimed. "You're here!"

As he looked up in surprise, I blurted out, "We have to talk!"

He shut off the buffer, studied my red, puffy face, and shook his head. "No, Becky," he said. "We have to pray."

He took my hand and led me into the first-grade Sunday school classroom where we sat down in little kiddie chairs. Ralph then asked: "Do you *want* to pray?"

I couldn't say yes fast enough.

"Do you want to ask Jesus to come into your life?"

"Oh, yes, yes," I cried out.

So right there on those little chairs, sitting with our knees tucked up under our chins, Ralph explained that he would begin the prayer, and I was to pray after him.

Ralph began slowly, "Dear Jesus . . ." Within just a few sentences I knew that everything pressuring me from the inside was going to come spilling out. And it did.

"Jesus," Ralph prayed, "I've been a sinner . . ."

Once Ralph got me started, I wasn't about to stop. I told God what an awful sinner I was. I told him I was sorry for all the things I had done. I admitted I had made a mess of my life and asked him to help clean it up. I prayed on and on, begging for help in every area of my life. I had heard the expression "pouring out your heart," and that's the best way to explain what I did. I emptied myself out before God. I spilled out my whole messed-up life in that little room.

And as I prayed, a steady, gentle stillness flowed over and through me like a soothing shower, washing down over my head and shoulders into my heart and right on down to my toes. As I continued to confess the wrong things I had done, the peace changed slowly to joy, and through my tears I wanted to laugh because it was all so wonderful.

I, Becky Jacobs, was praying to God, and he was listening—I could tell. He was there in that room, listening to me, loving me, forgiving me.

"Jesus . . ." Ralph was leading again and I was praying the words after him. "Please forgive me for all these things. Come into my life; make me a new person." That's what I wanted. Yes, to be a new person. "Come into my heart. Take over my heart and take over my life. I don't want to control it any longer. I want you in control. Fill me with your Holy Spirit right now, Lord."

And that's what happened. Ralph paraphrased a Scripture verse from 2 Corinthians, saying, "When someone becomes a Christian, he becomes a brand new person inside; the old things pass away and new things are begun!" And I knew it was true.

I was different. I could feel it—and God had done it.

I couldn't wait to get back to work and tell everyone. I stopped in the computer room first to tell two coworkers,

Tamara and Ruth. "You won't believe what just happened to me . . ."

They didn't say a word for the next five minutes as I whizzed through a summary account of my meeting with Ralph and a quick description of the joyous high I now felt. Then Tamara just shook her head and grinned, "You've been saved, Becky. I just don't believe it!"

I didn't understand what she meant, "saved." But I didn't stop to ask before I rushed out and told one of the salesmen what had happened. As a church-going Baptist, he nodded and said, "That's great, you've been 'born again.' "

That didn't make any more sense than "saved," but I had heard the term before, and it sure fit the way I felt.

I hurried on into Mrs. Felton's office and sat down in front of her desk. "Guess what just happened?" and concluded by using one of the new terms. "I guess I've been born again. I just know this is going to be the answer to my drinking problem."

Mrs. Felton smiled and nodded silently through my entire account. When I finished she said, "I'm so glad you've found something you think will help you, Becky. I must say, you certainly look different!"

I knew that had to be true. I had felt so uptight, so oppressed for weeks. I'd been depressed and irritable—with a countenance to match. Suddenly I felt so happy I couldn't wipe the smile off my face.

That wasn't the only obvious difference. That same afternoon, when the new switchboard operator wanted to take a break, I said, "Sure, Ellen, I'll be glad to sit in for you." Since I'd been promoted I'd done almost everything to avoid switchboard duty, so Ellen responded to my offer with an incredulous double take. "What's with you, Becky?" she wanted to know.

I told her all about what had happened, and the next day I told her more. And on Sunday, just three days later, she went with me to church, met Ralph, and made the same decision I had, to ask God to forgive and change her. I was ecstatic; now I had someone who could share my excitement and my new experience with me.

I practically bowled people over to tell them what had happened. Those I didn't get to talk to were soon asking other people, "What's with Becky?" It was obvious to everyone that I had changed.

What amazed and excited me the most wasn't the outward change people could notice but the inner change only I knew about.

Most amazing of all was the fact that I no longer craved alcohol. The moment I asked God to take control of my life the desire to drink that had directed my life for more than five years disappeared. The freedom was almost enough to make me giddy.

I went back to an AA meeting just to see if I could find Bill and tell him Jesus was a better answer than antibuse. He listened and seemed interested. I invited him to church with me, but I don't know what happened to him because he never showed up.

I, on the other hand, would show up at church any time the doors opened, and I met regularly with Ralph for Bible study and prayer. It almost seemed as if my craving for alcohol had been replaced by an insatiable desire to read my Bible, pray, and learn more about God.

It soon became obvious that I would have to move. Pam and I were now going in opposite directions. I told her what had happened to me, but she wanted nothing to do with it. So I began to look for a new place to live, and a new lifestyle.

I maintained most of my relationships at work, but after work my life quickly changed. Ralph began taking me to a Wednesday night Bible study and prayer group, where I found an immediate and new group of friends with whom I could socialize.

The life that had seemed so hopeless, so messed up, had turned 180 degrees and was changing faster than I could believe. I longed to write and tell John all my good news, but he was already on his way back across the country. I'd be able to tell him everything soon enough—face to face.

I could hardly wait.

CHAPTER 13

IN DIFFERENT WORLDS

The card from John came at the end of the first week of September. It said, "I'll be home the fourteenth. Can't wait to see you."

I read and reread the card a dozen times before the date hit me. *The fourteenth? That's the night of the Christian Businessmen's dinner!* Ralph had recruited me to go and sing with an informal choir that would provide the special music. I liked to sing and had enjoyed getting together with Ralph and his friends to learn a small repertoire of praise songs and gospel choruses.

As soon as I got the card, I called Ralph, intending to back out of the dinner. "That's going to be John's first night back in town," I told him.

"Why don't you invite John to come along?" he asked.

"I don't know." I somehow had a hard time picturing John at a Christian businessmen's dinner. *And yet,* I thought, *that might be a good chance for him to see the change in me.* "Maybe I will," I finally said.

By the fourteenth, my mind was made up, but as the afternoon waned, I wondered if I would even have a chance to ask John before I had to leave for the dinner. I put on a nice dress and was working on my makeup when the phone finally rang.

"I'm over at Pam's." The voice was John's. "And I found out you moved."

"Yeah, just last month. There was no way to let you know. I'm sorry."

"How do I find you?"

I gave him the directions and sat down to wait. I had

found an apartment—actually the upstairs of a house owned by an elderly widow. I shared the front entrance of the house, but for the first time in my life I wasn't sharing a place with anyone else. The apartment was all mine.

The moment I heard the motor outside I rushed to the window and saw the familiar turquoise pickup roll to a stop in the driveway. I was halfway down the steps by the time I heard a door slam, and I threw myself into John's arms before he got halfway up the sidewalk.

"Oh, I missed you!" I told him in the middle of a long embrace. "I'm so glad you're back!"

"I missed you, too," John responded as I heard another door slam. I released John and looked over to see another guy walking around the front of the truck.

"Becky," John said, "I'd like you to meet Brent. He was my college roommate, and he's gonna be staying a couple of days before he heads on down to San Diego."

I greeted him and Brent grinned. "I've heard a lot about you."

John took my arm. "What do you say we all go out and celebrate?"

"Oh, I almost forgot," I said. "I've got to leave for a meeting in about fifteen minutes."

John looked me over and I knew he was noting the dress as he said, "I wondered what was up." It may have been the first time he'd ever seen me in a dress outside of work hours.

"It's a dinner for local business people. Over at the Holiday Inn. You're both welcome to come."

"Do you have to go?"

"I promised I would."

"All right." John looked at Brent. "We'll go, and afterwards we'll go dancing at Tia Maria's and celebrate."

"Sure," I said. "That'll be great."

I didn't tell John about the singing. I figured that would be a surprise. I also figured he'd be proud of my singing and the changes in me.

I was partly right. John was completely surprised by what he found at the dinner. Everyone who stood at the microphone at the head table said something about "praising the Lord," enjoying our "Christian fellowship," feeling "the presence of the Holy Spirit," or some similar terminology. I saw John look at Brent and kind of roll his eyes in amusement when a smattering of "amens" or "praise the Lords" sounded around the room.

When I went and stood in the front with the rest of our little choir, I kept my eyes on John. I hoped he was listening to the words of the songs, "They'll Know We Are Christians by Our Love," and "He's Everything to Me." But the smile on his face seemed forced and I could tell by the disbelieving look he gave me when I returned to the table that he was puzzled by the whole scene.

"Well, this wasn't exactly the way I figured you'd meet Becky," he said to Brent as we walked out of the Holiday Inn at the close of the dinner. "But I did tell you she was crazy and unpredictable, didn't I?"

He and Brent laughed. I realized I had some serious explaining to do.

We found a table in the back of Tia Maria's, a Mexican restaurant with a bar and a dance floor. John and Brent ordered beers. I told the waitress, "Just ginger ale for me, thanks."

John gave me a funny look and I added, "I'm not drinking anymore."

"You're not?"

I shook my head. "No."

"When did this happen?" John wanted to know.

"It started when I decided I was an alcoholic."

"You are not!" John quickly replied. He seemed as intent on denying it for Brent's sake, or his own, as he was on convincing me.

"Well," I said, "I felt I was an alcoholic."

"Maybe you thought it, but you're no alcoholic, Becky."

I didn't argue but I just went on to tell John and Brent about how I'd turned to God, how my life was different now, and how I didn't even want to drink.

I expected John to be excited for me, to want what I'd found. He wasn't—he didn't.

He listened—probably because he could tell what had happened was important to me. But he acted uncomfortable and a little embarrassed as I talked so intensely about God in front of his friend Brent. Whenever I'd toss a Scripture verse into the conversation, he'd try to change the subject until I finally quit talking and decided to dance and just enjoy John's company again. I knew there would be more time to talk later.

Even in the days after Brent left John wasn't any more receptive to the spiritual things I wanted to tell him.

"Religion is just a crutch for weak people," he said. "If you were an alcoholic, maybe that was just your weakness. I don't know. If it helps you, fine. I don't need it."

I remained convinced that he did need it. I was reading and studying the Bible and learning what the Scriptures say about heaven and hell and eternal life. When Ralph showed me where the Bible said believers shouldn't marry unbelievers, I saw even more reason for convincing John. But the more I talked, the harder I pushed, the more resistant he got.

It was as if we were walking hand in hand down a path until we suddenly came to a crack in the earth—splitting our path right down the middle. We kept walking, holding hands over the crack, which gradually widened between us, but before long we were having to stretch to reach each other over the fissure.

I told John what I saw happening. "We're in different worlds, going in different directions. There's a chasm opening up between us, and if you don't cross over soon, John, it's going to separate us forever."

We both tried to ignore the increasing tension between us and continued to spend hours together every day, dinner every night, movies, dancing. Yet there was no denying our growing differences were tearing at our relationship.

We had at least one major conflict—the same one every night. When John would take me back to my apartment, or if we'd be at my apartment and bedtime came, he always wanted to stay, and I'd firmly insist he go home.

After a few nights of this, he finally exploded and demanded to know, "Why can't I stay?"

"Because it's not right," I said, "and it's part of what I believe."

"Then why didn't you believe that before?"

"I don't know," I replied. "But now that I'm reading the Bible, I do know that sleeping with you would be wrong."

"Who says it's wrong?"

I showed him a few verses I had found, but that only made him angrier, and he demanded to know where love fit into the picture.

That's when I turned to 1 Corinthians 13 and defined love for him: "Love is patient and kind . . ."

Moments later I heard his truck door slam and the tires squeal as he backed out of the driveway and raced off down the street. I cried as I prayed and asked God to make John see, to make John change. I was beginning to realize I couldn't change him.

One Sunday morning in Sunday school as we closed the hour by saying the Lord's Prayer together, the words *Our Father* suddenly stabbed me like a sword. Throughout the entire prayer I could think of nothing but my father, my parents, and how much pain I had caused them. By the time we got to *the glory forever* tears of remorse were coursing down my cheeks.

"Becky, what's wrong?" Ralph wanted to know.

"I think maybe I ought to go home and let my parents see the change in me." Just saying the word *home* made it sound so good, so appealing and secure.

"I think that's a good idea," Ralph said.

I sadly shook my head. "But how can I go home? I've gone home so many times, and it's always been a disaster. My mom and I have such awful fights. I always end up hurting them.

"Besides, I have a job," I added. "I was just home two

months ago, and I don't have the money for transportation across the country. I can't go."

Ralph gently put his hand on my shoulder. He understood much of my hesitation; in the weeks after I asked God to take over my life we'd talked a lot. I'd told him virtually everything about my life. I'd confessed all the wrong I had done, all the lies I had told, all the hurt I had caused, and he continually assured me, "God will forgive that, too, if you just ask him, Becky."

Now in the empty Sunday school room he said, "If God wants you to go home, he'll open up a way. Why don't you take the first step and see what happens?"

So that very afternoon I picked up the phone to call my parents. I held the receiver and stared at the numbers for the longest time thinking about the times I had called home from Wisconsin, from college. *This is different,* I told myself. *But each time I've talked to Mom about coming home, she's been more reluctant. We start fighting at a moment's notice. Maybe they won't even want me to come home this time. I wouldn't blame them.*

As I thought about these things I almost hung up. But then I thought of praying. "Lord, if you want me to go home, you've got to work this out." Slowly, deliberately, I began to dial Chicago.

"Hello," Dad answered. That was a good start; it wasn't Mom.

"It's Becky, Dad."

"I was just thinking about you, honey. We haven't heard from you in a while. How are you?"

So I told him—told him all about my turning to God, how I had stopped drinking, about how much I'd changed, and how excited I was to feel so different. He listened, now and then offering "Really?" "That's good," or "I'm glad" to keep me pouring out the details.

When I finished, there was a long pause, as if Dad could tell I was leading up to something. Finally I just said it. "Dad, I'd like to come home."

"When should we expect you?"

There had been no pause—no hesitancy. Just those immediate words of acceptance. I had never felt more loved than I felt in that moment. My father wanted his prodigal daughter to come home. And his only question was *when* I'd be there. He wanted to be ready.

A million thoughts flashed through my mind. *Home. I'm going home. My dad wants me to come home! I'll be able to show him and Mom I have changed. I'm going home. But how? When?*

"I don't know," I said, pondering Dad's question. "I've got a lot of details to work out. Probably in about two weeks."

"Wonderful," Dad replied. "We'll see you in two weeks."

After I hung up the phone, I just sat reflecting on everything that had happened. I picked up the phone again and called Mrs. Felton at home. She had really begun to count on me at the office, so I didn't think she would be very happy about my plans.

I told her I felt I needed to go home to let my folks see how I had changed, and she said she thought that would be a good idea. She had seen the change and realized how important it was to me for my parents to see it, too. She immediately offered to give me a one- or two-month leave of absence, but I would need to spend the next couple of weeks training the other girls in the office how to cover my duties.

When I hung up from talking to her, my mind was racing again. I couldn't believe how quickly things were falling into place. I would have to sell my little car so I could pay off my credit union loan before I left town, and I still had to figure out how I could *afford* to go home! But two major hurdles had been crossed in two brief phone calls, so I felt certain the Lord would work out the rest.

I was going home!

That very week a salesman who called occasionally stopped at my desk at the office to chat. He asked what was new with me. So I told him everything—about finding God, about quitting drinking, and about my plans to go home to Chicago as soon as I could find a way.

"You're not going to believe this," the man said when I

finished, "but I've got a friend who has been looking for someone to drive his motor home back to Chicago for him. It's parked right now at my place up in Oakland. I'll give him a call tonight and see what he says."

A couple of days later I got a telegram from the owner of the motor home, authorizing me to drive his vehicle across the country. He was even going to pay for the gas.

Just two days before I planned to leave, someone at the dealership saw my For Sale sign and bought my car. He paid my asking price without a question. All the hurdles were crossed.

John drove me up to Oakland to get the motor home. I felt none of the hysteria I had felt about leaving at the airport back in July. He hadn't argued about my decision to go home. In fact, I had been a little hurt that he hadn't been any more reluctant to see me go. Yet he seemed to understand how important it was for me to see my parents and for them to see the new me.

Ralph had been planning a visit with his family back in Wisconsin, so he volunteered to go with me and share the driving of the twenty-six-foot motor home. When one of us slept, the other one drove, and with the only stops being for gas and occasional meals, the miles and two-thirds of a continent rolled by quickly—the Sierras, the flat deserts of Nevada and Utah, the Rockies, and the endless plains.

There was a lot of time to think. I recalled the excitement I had felt when I first headed west. Fiddling with the radio, I remembered the words I had adopted as my personal fight song:

Somehow, someday, we need just one victory
   and we're on our way
Prayin' for it all day and fightin' for it all night
Give us just one victory and it will be all right.

I had spent two years in California fighting for some sort of victory, some sense of self-worth. I had succeeded in business, only to see that accomplishment crumble away when my personal life caved in. Now God had given me the victory I had been searching for, and my whole life was beginning to fall into place.

I still had some problems to work out, but the farther east I drove, the more certain I was that this homecoming would be different because I was different. Everything *would* be all right.

I could hardly wait to get home and share my victory with my parents and friends.

CHAPTER 14

GOING HOME

Only three days after we left Oakland, I dropped off Ralph at his parents' and drove down to Madison to visit my sister.

It was Friday afternoon when I pulled that huge motor home into the parking lot at my sister's apartment. Between the time I parked and when I knocked at Susie's apartment door, an idea hit me.

"Becky, what are you doing here?" Susie exclaimed as we embraced.

"How would you like to drive to Chicago tonight in a motor home? You could spend the weekend and fly back in time to work Monday."

"Sure," she said. "I'm always up for a weekend at home. Did you say a motor home?"

She laughed when she looked over my shoulder and saw it in the parking lot. "You can explain while I pack a suitcase, and then we can get this party rolling."

I decided I would wait to tell her I had quit drinking. There would be plenty of time to talk in the two hours it would take us to reach Chicago.

But the subject of the changes in my life didn't come up before we had pulled onto Interstate 90 and headed toward Illinois. Up ahead I noticed a man climbing out of his van on the shoulder of the highway. He staggered a little, raised his hands in the air, shouted something as we approached, and then fell flat on his face just as we passed him.

My first thought was that he was having a heart attack. I quickly wheeled the motor home over and rolled to a stop. I was opening the door and climbing out before Susie asked, "What's going on?"

"That man needs help," I shouted as I jumped down to the gravel and began sprinting back along the roadway. I could hear the crunch of the gravel behind me and knew Susie was running to keep up. I don't know whether or not she heard me praying out loud as I ran. "Help me, Jesus! Please help me!"

When I reached the man he was sitting and holding his chest and seemed very out of breath. I felt sure he was going to die.

"What's wrong?" I asked, kneeling beside him.

"I think it's a heart attack," he gasped.

I didn't know a bit of first aid, but I knew in an instant that the most important thing I could do for him was to tell him how he could know Jesus before he died and went into eternity.

So I asked, "Do you know Jesus?"

"What are you doing?" Susie looked at me like I'd gone insane.

But I didn't respond to her. I looked instead at the man sitting there in the gravel and told him, "If you want to know that you're going to heaven if you should die, all you have to do is ask Jesus to come into your heart and forgive you for all your sins and you'll receive eternal life."

"He needs medical help," Susie screamed. "Not a sermon! I'll try to flag down someone with a CB."

The man acted like he felt a little better, so I helped him to his feet and into his van. Then I drove the van up to the motor home and helped the man inside so he could lie on a bed until an ambulance arrived.

An eighteen-wheeler stopped and while Susie explained the situation to the trucker and waited for him to radio the nearest police station, I got out my Bible and read Scriptures to this man. I desperately wanted him to experience the same kind of peace and renewal I'd found two months earlier. As we talked, the man began to relax and soon we prayed together, much as Ralph and I had, and he asked Christ into his heart to control his life.

We'd just finished praying when the State Patrol and the paramedics pulled up and rushed the man off to the nearest hospital. The patrolman took my name and address to forward any information about the man's health to me later. I was to be pleasantly surprised a month later to receive a note from the man's wife, thanking me for praying with her husband and telling me that their whole family had begun to live Christian lives as a result of that incident on the side of the road. The man himself had suffered only a severe case of indigestion complicated by a large overdose of Maalox.

I didn't know any of this, of course, when I climbed back into the motor home and started on down the road again with a very bewildered sister. The time seemed right to explain everything that had happened since I'd seen her last. She listened as I told her about my conclusion that I was an alcoholic and how God had provided a wonderful way out for me—that I was a different person now.

By the time we reached the suburbs of Chicago I felt Susie understood what I was saying. But I didn't think she was sure how much to believe. I'd have to show her I'd really changed.

My mind raced and my heart pounded with excitement as I turned onto the street where my parents lived, where I'd grown up. Seeing the same familiar trees and the same familiar houses triggered doubts I hadn't felt for weeks. *Nothing has changed except me,* I thought. *Is that going to be enough?*

My parents' accepting hugs helped ease the doubts. I felt a warmth from them I hadn't felt in years—maybe because I felt a warmth *for* them again. They exclaimed their surprise at having Susie home, too. And they *oohed* and *aahed* over the motor home I had parked in the driveway, impressed with my ability to get it clear across the country and with the responsibility I'd been given. Then we retreated into the house, where Mom insisted on fixing us a late dinner, while I gave them a blow-by-blow description of everything that had happened to me since I'd been home in July. I concluded by saying, "I'm a different person now. The Lord has changed me. And the real reason I came home this time was to let you see how much I've changed."

"That's wonderful, dear. And we're glad you've come home," my mom assured me. But, like Susie, she sounded a little doubtful, and I didn't blame her for that. She seemed willing to give me a chance to prove myself, and I was grateful for that. I determined to show her I had indeed changed.

I saw more doubt in her eyes later that day when I told her I was going to my old "stomping grounds" to see all my friends that night. But she didn't say anything.

The first night with the old gang proved easier than I'd expected. Everyone gathered at a friend's house and we just sat around laughing and talking. Drinks were offered and a few people laughed when I told them I didn't drink anymore. No one laughed, though, when I explained by saying I'd become a born-again Christian and quickly summarized the recent spiritual changes in my life. There was merely an awkward silence for a few moments, and then someone launched the conversation in another direction. I didn't feel any pressure to drink, and when someone suggested going out to dinner the next night, I quickly agreed.

We met in an expensive dining room of a local hotel. When some of the other girls ordered something from the bar before dinner, I abstained. When wine was ordered with dinner, however, I decided one glass wouldn't hurt anything.

The goblet of white wine the waiter brought was huge, more than twice as big as a standard wine glass. And that wine, the first alcohol I'd had in weeks, tasted wonderful to me. I had to sip it slowly and fight the urge to order a second.

I went home very proud of the fact that I had controlled my drinking for the first time I could remember. It gave me a lot of confidence in my newfound willpower.

When Penny called the next day to say a few people would

be going out dancing that night, I said I'd go as long as we didn't go to our old drinking spot, Faces. I felt there would be too many memories, too many temptations there.

"How about going back to the hotel?" she asked. "There's a dance floor in the bar there."

"Sure," I said, thinking about that big goblet of wine again. "That would be fine with me."

That night, when I finished my goblet of wine I decided, *I'll have just one more. This wine isn't really going to affect me.* But the second big goblet gave me a nice buzz, and it took all the determination I could muster not to order another.

The clock said 12:30 when I got home. *That's only 9:30 in California*, I thought. *I'll give John a call.*

I walked to the kitchen phone so I wouldn't disturb my folks, but before I dialed I opened the counter door under the sink. Sure enough, there was a big jug of wine. *I'll just have another small glass while I'm talking to John, and then I'll be off to bed.*

So I poured a glass and dialed.

John told me about his day—and I poured myself another glass of wine and told him about my day. He said he missed me, and I told him I missed him more. Then I poured myself still another glass. The longer we talked, the more lonesome I got. And the more I drank. The next thing I knew I heard John shouting through the phone, "Becky! Becky! Are you still there?"

As my head cleared, I realized I had dozed off and the receiver had fallen to my lap. "Sorry, John, what were you saying?" I asked.

"You fell asleep, didn't you?"

I denied the accusation. "I'm okay. Just too tired to concentrate I guess."

"Becky! You're drunk." He'd known me too long not to recognize the usual symptoms.

"I am not!"

"You are, too!" There was irritation in his voice, not

because I was drunk, but because I hadn't been willing to drink with him.

"I'll call you again soon; I'm going to bed," I said sharply. "And I'm not drunk!"

When I hung up the phone and looked at the empty wine jug sitting on the floor beside me, I knew I was, and I cried myself to sleep.

When I got up late the next morning, Mom asked me if I had been drinking. I wanted to say no, but then I realized she might have found the empty wine jug where I had put it in the back of the cabinet. I really did want to be honest with my mother, to prove to her that I'd changed.

"Yes, I drank some wine," I admitted.

"Becky," she said, "if you're an alcoholic, you shouldn't drink any."

The next instant we were arguing again, but as soon as I realized it, I bit my tongue, told Mom I was sorry, and fled to the bathroom to regain my composure. *She makes me so mad,* I told myself through my tears. *Maybe we won't ever be able to get along.*

I began to pray. "Lord, you gotta help me with my mother. I don't want to fight with her. I want a new relationship, a caring, loving relationship."

The tone of my prayer changed from pleading to accusing as I changed the subject. "What happened last night, God? I thought you took away all the desire to drink, but I was drunk again."

I felt angry and disillusioned with God. Then it hit me. God really had taken away my desire to drink—unless I drank. Then the alcohol took control.

Mom was right. As an alcoholic, I couldn't drink at all. For me there was no such thing as moderation, and that thought scared me. I realized for the first time how different my life was going to have to be.

Penny and Wendy had promised to come by and take me out with some other friends again that next evening. So after dinner with my family, I tried to call to confirm the plans. Wendy's line was busy. So was Penny's. *Talking to each other, no doubt,* I concluded.

As I helped Mom dry the dinner dishes I stopped periodically to pick up the phone and dial again, but their phones were still busy. Eight o'clock came—the time they had said they would pick me up. Eight o'clock passed. I called again. No answer at Wendy's. Penny's dad answered. "She's not here," he said. "She left half an hour ago and I don't expect her back until late."

"Thank you," I said, and slowly hung up the phone. Then I slumped down in a chair and laid my head in my arms on the top of the kitchen table and began to cry. "They aren't coming," I said aloud and I heard my mother's footsteps come up behind me. I felt her hand rest on my shoulder.

My friends weren't coming for me. They wouldn't be coming. That realization hurt, but the tears weren't merely tears of pain. I was grieving, because the moment Penny's father hung up and I heard the phone line go dead something died inside me. In that instant I knew that my past was gone. The old Becky Jacobs was gone.

"Maybe it's for the best," Mom said, with her hand still resting gently on my shoulder.

I knew she was right. I remembered Ralph saying, "When a person becomes a Christian, old things pass away and all things become new." I knew without a doubt that that was what was happening to me. While I didn't want to go back to the old life—I wanted to be a new person—I felt a sudden sadness that only intensified my tears. My friends were part of my old life. Yet I still loved them. Their love and acceptance had been the most important thing in my life for so long, and it hurt deeply to realize our relationship might never be the same.

I don't know if Mom understood why I was crying. She didn't say anything, but she put her arms around me and held me. And I *felt* understood—and loved—and accepted.

It was a new, wonderful feeling.

EPILOGUE

I had come back to Illinois with the full intention of staying only a month or two, and then heading back to California to my old job and to John.

As the weeks passed, I realized things at home had never been better. The extent of the change surprised even me, and before long I knew my folks realized I'd changed, too. They acted a little wary of my constant Bible quoting and my out-loud prayers, but they obviously felt as good as I did about our new family harmony. I began to consider a longer stay—if I could find a job that would give me reason to stay in Chicago.

One day, on a lark, I decided to drop by the high school just to say hello to some of my old teachers. The first one I found was Mr. Rioni, who was now an assistant principal. I asked him if he wanted to check my purse for cigarettes, and we both laughed. He acted genuinely glad to see me, so when he asked me to tell him what had been happening in my life, I gave him the whole story—that I'd dropped out of college, moved to California, gotten a good job, but had become an alcoholic. I told him about my spiritual rebirth and how I'd come home to show my parents that I'd changed. I told him I was thinking about staying in Chicago if I could find a job—maybe something working with teenagers. "I want to do something to help keep kids from making the same mistakes I made," I concluded.

"I'm glad things are starting to work out for you," he said. "But about this idea of looking for a job to help kids—that sounds to me like maybe you're on a guilt trip." Then seeing the serious look on my face, he laughed and added, "But then again, maybe a guilt trip's good for you."

And I laughed.

After I'd said good-bye to Mr. Rioni, I looked in on my favorite school secretary, Mrs. Hughes. I hadn't seen her in four years, so I was a little surprised she remembered me. She listened with real interest as I told my story once again.

When I told her I was interested in working with kids, she told me about a national organization called Youth for Christ, which had local chapters called Campus Life Clubs in several Chicago area schools. "They meet every week to talk about kids' problems and what the Bible has to say about those problems," she explained. "The guy who heads it up is a school guidance counselor named Roger Tirabassi. I've got his number right here if you want to use my phone and give him a call."

So I called right from Mrs. Hughes's office and for the third time that day told my story. Roger then told me about his organization. He explained that the purpose of Campus Life was to help high school kids understand that to live a healthy, balanced life they had to include the spiritual along with their social, intellectual, and physical lives. In addition to regular meetings to talk about problems and the Bible, the group did things like take trips to Florida and Colorado. I could hardly believe such an organization existed. When Roger said they were always looking for volunteer staff people I was ready to sign on. All that remained was to find a paying job so I could stay in Chicago and volunteer with Campus Life.

I had barely hung up after agreeing to stop and meet Roger sometime soon, when another former teacher, Mr. Bradford, stopped in the office. Once more I told my story and shared my desire to do something to help young people.

This man also listened with interest and when I finished he said, "I just heard about a new position the school board is trying to fill. It's a social work job to help high school kids with drug and alcohol problems."

My hopes were rising so fast I wasn't even deterred when

Mr. Bradford added, "But I'm sure they're looking for someone with experience and a college degree in social work."

"It sounds perfect," I exclaimed. "Where can I apply?"

"Well," he said, "you can call Mr. Adams over at the school board office."

"Mr. Jack Adams?" I asked.

"Yes. Why? Do you know him?"

"He was an assistant principal when I was in junior high school," I informed him.

"Well, his office is doing the hiring for this position. I suppose it would at least be worth a call."

So again I used Mrs. Hughes's phone. Mr. Adams remembered me and I told him my story. When I finished I said, "Because of my own personal experience with drugs and alcohol, I think I'd be a good candidate for that new job you have."

"I'm sorry, Becky," he said. "But one of the requirements is a four-year college degree."

"But couldn't I at least apply?"

"Well," he hesitated, "you can apply if you want, I guess. Do you have any local references?"

My local reputation wasn't exactly what I needed to win this job. I needed someone who believed in me, who understood what had happened to me. "I've been away for several years," I said. Then I had a thought. "There is one person; he's a guidance counselor in the school system, Roger Tirabassi."

"Okay, that's a start," Mr. Adams said. "You can come by and fill out an application if you like, but I certainly can't promise anything."

That afternoon visit to my old high school became another turning point in my life—almost as significant as the day of my deposition back in August. Several things happened as a result of the contacts made in Mrs. Hughes's office.

Incredibly, after numerous interviews and repeating my story to school board officials and other community leaders, I got the social work job. When they waived their requirement of a college degree and offered me the position, I sent my apology and resignation to Mrs. Felton. It wasn't easy giving up the success I'd found in California.

However, I soon discovered greater satisfaction and a higher victory in my new job. It was especially heartening to realize that God was using all those wasted years and all those wasted opportunities. Those experiences became my passport, my credibility as I tried to steer other teenagers away from my mistakes. It was a marvelous thing to have the chance to make a positive difference in other peoples' lives.

But more than a job came out of that afternoon. I soon met Roger Tirabassi face to face and immediately got involved as a volunteer with Campus Life. This additional attempt to help others ended up helping me most of all. The Campus Life staff quickly filled all my needs for friendship and acceptance. They also became my spiritual mentors as we worked together, studied the Bible, and developed strategies for sharing our faith with high school kids.

As I continued to grow stronger in my faith, my parents became more and more impressed with the changes in me. Mom began going to a Wednesday evening prayer meeting and Bible study with me at a church in a nearby town. Then one Saturday morning, as we sat together at our kitchen table, she prayed and asked God to take control of her life in the same way he had done for me. As Mom began to change, Dad became curious and started going with us on Wednesdays. One evening he went forward and prayed to ask God to take control of his life as well, and our family life changed forever.

Through all this time I kept hoping and praying that John would decide to make the same commitment to God that I had made. At the end of the year I flew back to California for a few days to see my old friends and to show John how much I still cared about him. But the chasm between us seemed to be growing wider and wider.

During the months that followed we kept writing—and I kept praying. That next summer he came east to see me, and we went out together every night. While he'd drink beer, I'd sip on a soft drink, and we'd go over and over our differences.

The next to the last night of his visit we took a midnight canoe ride on a nearby lake. The night felt so warm and romantic that we set our paddles down and just drifted in the silvery, shimmering light of the full summer moon, gentle waves lapping softly against the hull. We were silent for a long time before John spoke the words I had longed to hear him say.

"Becky, I want to ask you to marry me. But . . ."

We both knew there was a but.

He continued. "But if I married you, there'd be something I couldn't give you that you want in a husband. I can't believe what you believe."

We argued for a while, but I think we both knew it was no use. Finally we paddled back to shore with nothing resolved.

THE NEXT NIGHT, John's last before he planned to fly back to California, we went out to eat again. This time, though, when John ordered something to drink, so did I. When he ordered a second, so did I. Before long I was rip-roaring drunk and very angry at John for letting me get drunk—and at myself for not being stronger.

I cried myself to sleep that night and awakened the next morning feeling very weak, betrayed, and alone. I wasn't strong enough to stand alone, and the man I loved didn't care enough about me, didn't respect me enough not to drink around me, even though he knew I was an alcoholic. Realizing both those things, I also realized there was no hope for us. Our relationship was over. But it still hurt.

The next morning we made a quiet trip to the airport and said a somber good-bye. I never saw John again.

But just as God had replaced my California job with a more fulfilling one and had given me a whole new set of Christian friendships, he provided someone to take John's place. A little over a year after that eventful afternoon in Mrs. Hughes's office when I'd made the contacts that led to a new career, new friendships, and a new family, one more life-changing event resulted: Roger Tirabassi asked me to marry him.

A lot has happened since then. Roger and I did get married, and we now have a beautiful son. I worked part-time for several years leading a Campus Life Club in the very high school I attended as a teenager. Ironically, though I wasn't a member of the Central High School faculty, I even served for several years as the school's cheerleading coach.

Today I'm still devoting my life to working with young people who struggle as I did with issues of popularity, peer pressure, self-image, and family tensions. I want others to understand that drug and alcohol abuse don't solve any of those things; they only complicate them and make everything worse.

The answer I found, the only answer to my problems, was turning my life over to Christ—not that he somehow waves a celestial wand and life becomes instantly perfect, but he gives the strength, hope, and help one needs to cope with the problems.

I'll always be an alcoholic. But God gives me the strength never to drink. And that, for me, is a life-changing victory.

A Final Word from Becky

I have shared this story with you, but not because I'm proud of it. The truth is it's embarrassing and painful to expose my weaknesses and publicly admit my mistakes. I do it because I've worked with teenagers for the last fourteen years and I've found a great many who are headed down the same path I took. Some are just starting out; others have gone far down the road. But I have yet to find one person who has found lasting happiness or success by losing himself or herself in alcohol, drugs, or premarital sex.

I would never want to go back and relive the times you've read about. In writing this book, I hope I can keep at least one other person, maybe you, from making the same mistakes.

Perhaps you're thinking, *No way! Not me! I'll never go that far!* Maybe you won't. But you could. I know because I would have said the same thing.

"Become an alcoholic? Me? Never! You gotta be kidding!"

"Destroy my relationship with my family? They are too important to me."

"Dump all my moral values? It won't happen!"

But all those things did happen.

I didn't make a big conscious decision to do them; there was never a big fork in the road where I had to decide whether to be an alcoholic or a teetotaler, or where I had to choose once and for all between family and friends, or between the moral high road and the moral low road.

It happened with small decisions, little choices, that added up to determine the direction of my life. Those choices took me down a dead-end road where I finally had to stop and face the ugly fact that all those things I'd said would never happen had already happened.

Looking back, I realize there were many points where I could have made different choices. Hindsight makes it easy to see those times when something or someone was calling me to change, to turn, to steer clear of a mistake I was about to make. Why didn't I make a different choice? Sometimes I resented the interference of those who were concerned about me. I was proud. I didn't want to face the shame of letting others know what my life was really like.

Maybe you have some different excuses for continuing your own way, for making little decisions you know aren't right but don't seem very wrong.

If so—if you're somewhere on that road I was on—I've written this book for you. Not just to warn you about the possible dangers ahead, but because the answers and the victory you're looking for lie on a different road.

This past summer I drove down Highway 1, the Pacific Coast Highway, and I looked out over the Pacific Ocean again. I no longer saw an endless, bottomless ocean I wanted to escape into. I saw instead beauty and peace.

My life, which once seemed so empty and hopeless, is now filled to overflowing with family, friends, good memories, and years of rewarding work. All because of what happened ten years ago when instead of turning the wheel of my car and plunging over the cliff, I turned to Jesus Christ and prayed to ask him into my life. And that one decision, that one victory is still the biggest motivating factor in my life. Jesus became my friend and my partner. He continues to heal my hurts and share his strength when I'm weak. He has given me a place to belong. Now and forever.

And he wants to do the same for you.

There is a Scripture, Psalm 40, that says, "He lifted me out . . . of the mud and mire." After reading my story, you can see that's what Jesus did for me. And if Jesus can change someone like me, he will gladly do it for you.

I tell my story because I want you to know there are answers to your questions. There is healing for your hurts.

There is hope for your fears. And there is forgiveness for your failures.

In my heart I believe that only Jesus offers all these things. Only Jesus can enable you to be the person you want to be. He simply waits and knocks at the door of your heart. All you have to do is open it. Don't be afraid.

There is no secret in coming to Jesus. We need to admit our sins, accept who he is and what he did for us personally when he died on the cross, and then ask him into our hearts. If you are ready and willing to give your heart to Christ and begin a new life (2 Corinthians 5:17), then I would encourage you to pray this prayer.

Dear Lord,

I can't run or hide any longer from my problems. Please help me. Come into my life. Forgive me of my sins. I need you. Please begin, even today, to bring healing and happiness back into my life. Show me what to do, whom to talk to, whom I can trust. . . . Please fill me up to overflowing with your powerful and supernatural Holy Spirit.

Amen

Now!!! Get out a Bible, paper, and pencil, and spend time with God daily! You can do it!

If You Prayed That Prayer ...

*I*f you prayed that prayer or would like more information on Becky Tirabassi's ministry and/or her other books, just write to her at:

MY PARTNER MINISTRIES
Box 8862
Orange, CA 92664

If you are interested in getting involved in a local Youth for Christ program, write for more information to:

YOUTH FOR CHRIST
Box 419
Wheaton, IL 60189

If you need help with a drug or alcohol-related problem, please call NEW LIFE TREATMENT CENTERS at 1-800-227-LIFE for local and national hotline numbers, centers, personal counsel, or advice.